MW01593413

← Wumen
(Meridian Gate)

Inner Golden River →

← Taihemen(Gate of Great Harmony) and Golden River Bridges

↑ Golden River Bridges

↑ Bronze lion in front of the Gate of Great Harmony

↑ Taihedian (Hall of Great Harmony)(side view)

Bronze crane →

↑ Taihedian (Hall of Great Harmony)

Jia Liang (Standard Measure)→

↓ Huge carved stone pavement
  behind Baohedian
  (Hall of Preserving Harmony)

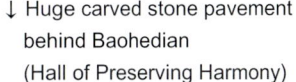

← Gilt copper vat (detail)

↑ Bronze tortoise

← Qianqingmen
(Gate of Heavenly Purity)

惟精惟一道積于厥躬

弘敷五典無輕民事惟難

正大光明

克寬克仁皇建其有極

表正萬邦慎嚴身修思永

↑ Interior view of the Palace of Heavenly Puritty

Gilt copper lion →

↓ Snowy Changyin'ge (Pavilion of Pleasant Sounds)

↓ Huangjidian
(Hall of Imperial Supremacy)

↑ Ningshoumen
(Gate of Tranquility and Longevity)

← Interior view of
Yangxingdian(Hall of
Cultivating Nature)

↓ Arrow Pavilion

Guhuaxuan →
vilion of Ancient Glory)

← Nine-Dragon Screen
(detail)

↑ Wenyuan'ge
(Pavilion of the Source of Literature)

↓ Board inscribed with characters
Longzongmen
(Gate of Great Ancestors)

↑ Yuhuage (Yuhua Pavilion)

↑ Painted lacquer screen with auspicious
design in gold tracery

↓ Chuxiugong
(Palace of Gathering Excellence)

↑ East chamber of Yangxindian
(Hall of Mental Cultivation)

↓ Wanchunting(Ten Thousand Spring Pavilion)

↓ Yujingting
  (Pavilion of Imperial Landscape)

↓ Gilt copper elephant

↑ Duixiushan(Hill of Accumulated Refinement)

↑ Tianyimen (Tian Yi Gate)

← Shenwumen
(Gate of Martial Spirit)

Corner Tower →

ACROSS
THE THRESHOLD OF
THE FORBIDDEN CITY

By Feng Linying

Translated by
Wang Heping and Liu Chang

Morning Glory Publishers

图书在版编目（CIP）数据

走进紫禁城/冯林英著；王和平，刘畅译．
—北京：朝华出版社，2003．11
ISBN 7 – 5054 – 0906 – 9

Ⅰ．走… Ⅱ．①冯…②王…③刘… Ⅲ．故宫—
简介—英文 Ⅳ．K928.74

中国版本图书馆 CIP 数据核字（2003）第 101763 号

走进紫禁城

作　　者	冯林英	
翻　　译	王和平　刘　畅	
责任编辑	凌舒昉	
封面设计	吴朝洪	
责任印制	赵　岭	
出版发行	朝华出版社	
社　　址	北京市车公庄西路 35 号　　　邮政编码　100044	
电　　话	（010）68433166（总编室）	
	（010）68413840/68433213（发行部）	
传　　真	（010）88415258（发行部）	
印　　刷	北京顺义振华印刷厂	
经　　销	中国国际图书贸易总公司	
开　　本	大 32 开　　　　　字　　数　100 千字	
印　　数	0001 – 5000 册　　　印　　张　7	
版　　次	2004 年 1 月第 1 版第 1 次印刷	
装　　别	平	
书　　号	ISBN 7 – 5054 – 0906 – 9/G·0312	
	002500	

The publishers thank Mr. Matthew Harris for checking the English transcriptions of Chinese texts.

Author' Acknowledgments:

I wish to express my gratitude to Mr. Xu Qixian, a senior researcher of the Palace Museum for his enthusiastic aid and detailed explanation on special Imperial Court terms of the Ming and Qing Dynasties.

Editor: Ling Shufang
Written by: Feng linying
Translated by: Wang Heping, Liu Chang
Photographer: Feng Linying
Illustrator: Feng Yuying
Layout Designers: Wu Chaohong
Cover Designer: Wu Chaohong

First Edition 2004

Across the Threshold of the Forbidden City

ISBN 7—5054—0906—9/G · 0312

©Morning Glory Publishers
Published by Morning Glory Publishers
35 Chegongzhuang Xilu, Beijing 100044, China
E-mail Addresses: zhzb@ mail. cibtc. com. cn
Distributed by China International Book Trading Corporation
35 Chegongzhuang Xilu, Beijing 100044, China
Printed in the People's Republic of China

Prelude

Across the border of China is a land of ancient wonders that has been too often misunderstood for us to pass without stare. Across the wall of the Forbidden City is a spirit of beauty and power who has been too long veiled for us to stare without touch. Five hundred year is long but also short, giving merely the last glance of the imperial pedigree onto the bounded but deemed boundless empire. Architecture is rich but yet pale, in telling days and nights of all the dwellers inside invisible embrace of the emperor.

Across the threshold of the Forbidden City, across the threshold of history, as reading a dust covered book, read this one. The first page, the reality of relics. The second, the stories behind. Grandeur halls and squares outline magnificent ceremonies, while delicate decorations depict luxurious but lonely lives of the ladies and subordinate buildings murmur humble whispers of servants. The book is aimed to be a guide and a company. With it, you will be with a tool to remove the dust of time; opening it, you are crossing the threshold of the Forbidden City into yesterday. And the last bar of the prelude, look, fell, read and then dream.

Content

1. Building and Scale of the Forbidden City

In the 4th year after Emperor Yongle who was titled posthumously by his successor as Chengzu mounted the throne in Ming dynasty (1406), he decided to change the city of Beiping, literally Peace of the North, into Beijing, the northern capital of the empire. The reconstruction was largely completed in the year the 18th year of Yongle period (1420).

Beijing City in Ming dynasty had a structural system of 4 folds of envelopes, the Forbidden City, the Imperial City, the inner city and the outer city. The Forbidden City in Chinese was named after *Ziwei* Constellation, where it was believed the God of Heaven lived and ordinary people were forbidden to enter without permission. Outside the Forbidden City is the Imperial City of a perimeter of 18 *li* (9 kilometers). There were 4 gates (or *men* in Chinese) in the middle of each side of the quasi-square city, the gate of *Daming* in the south, the gate of *Di'an* in the north, *Dong'anmen* in the east and *Xi'anmen* in the west. The inner city is the space surrounding the Imperial City, which altogether had 9 gates in 4 directions, *Dongzhimen, Chaoyangmen, Chongwenmen, Zhengyangmen, Xuanwumen, Fuchengmen, Xizhimen, Deshengmen,* and *Andingmen*. The City moat is still enveloping the inner city. The construction of the outer city in Ming dynasty was only set up partially in the southern areas because of financial problems, thus only 7 gates along the wall were built, which include *Dongbianmen, Guangqumen, Zuo'anmen, You'anmen, Yongdingmen, Guang'anmen* and *Xibianmen*. The City moat was also used to guard the city.

According to the record in the historic book *The Rite of Zhou Dynasty*, which reads (when facing the south) *Left the Ancestor Temple, Right the Altars to the Gods and Earth and Grain, Front the Court and Back the Market,* the Forbidden City was designed to have temples, governmental offices and a market traditionally at each direction. Besides, the Jingshan Hill is located to the north of the Palace as a back screen of the imperial building complex.

The Forbidden City covers a land of 720,000 square meters, and is surrounded by a 10 meters high and nearly 3.5 kilometers long wall. On the Wall, there are 4 gateways facing the 4 directions, *Wumen* (Meridian Gate) to the South, *Donghuamen*

(East Glorious Gate) to the east, *Xuanwumen* to the north and *Xihuamen* (West Glorious Gate) to the west. In the successive Qing dynasty, the name of the north gate was changed into *Shenwumen* (Gate of Martial Spirit) to avoid using the character *Xuan* which appeared in the name of Emperor Kangxi. At each turning corner of the wall, is a most exquisite structure, the corner tower. The 52 meters wide moat outside the Forbidden City is also a part of the defending system.

Legend tells that there were all together 9,999 and a half square bays inside the Forbidden City, but the remaining sums up to over 8,700. All the buildings were arranged into courtyards along the middle axis of the capital, basically symmetrical. Such regular and tidy layout decorated with glazed tile works gives a splendid and magnificent view. If appreciated from outside, the ripples are slightly and tranquilly creasing the reflections of aloft corner tower of gorgeous colors and the plain gray wall in the moat water. The Forbidden City condenses characteristics of Chinese historic architecture. It remains most of the original layout in Ming dynasty after centuries of repair, change and rebuild.

2. Outer and Inner Court of the Forbidden City

Inside the Forbidden City, there are basically two functional areas, i. e. the outer and inner court areas. The outer court area was for the emperors and his minister to hold ceremonies and political activities, while the inner court was for family affairs and abode of the emperor and his concubines and children. Some political affairs were also dealt with in the inner court.

The outer court begins at *Wumen* (Meridian Gate), and ends right in front of *Qianqingmen* (Gate of Heavenly Purity). Within the area, stand the 3 main halls of the imperial palace, *Taihedian* (Hall of Great Harmony), *Zhonghedian* (Hall of Middle

Harmony) and *Baohedian* (Hall of Preserving Harmony). To the east are *Wenhuadian* (Hall of Literary Glory), *Wenyuan'ge* (Pavilion of Source of Literature) and *Neigedatang* (Grand Secretariat Office), and to the west, *Wuyingdian* (Hall of Military Eminence), *Renzhi* Hall, etc.

Wenhuadian (Hall of the Literary Glory), was the hall for the civil officials and used to be the palace for the crown princes in Ming dynasty, and the place for canon banquet in Qing dynasty. Canon banquet took place on fixed dates, and the emperor and his ministers were to attend. Specially designated ministers were asked to narrate the traditional canonical works, *the Four Books* and *the Five Classics*, and tea and a banquet was to be held afterward. In 1438, the 3rd year of emperor Zhengtong's rein, the emperor commanded to script all the names of officials both civil and military in this hall for the purpose of assessment.

Wenyuange, (the Pavilion of Literary Source), was built as an imperial library. It was dedicated to storing the greatest series of books and the greatest reference books in Qianlong period, *Si Ku Quan Shu* (*the Complete Library in Four Divisions* over 79,000 volumes) and *Gujin Tushu Jicheng* (*Collection of Ancient and Modern Books*). The Cabinet Hall, also called Grand Secretariat Office where cabinet members held offices was situated to the south of *Wenyuange*.

Wuyingdian (Hall of Military Eminences) was a palace for the emperor's fasting days, and where he met his ministers during that time. The back hall of the complex was the working space for court painters. At the fall of Ming dynasty, Li Zicheng, the chief of the rebels, mounted the throne in this courtyard, and the regency Dorgun in the early years of Qing dynasty also handled affairs here. Later *Wuyingdian* was used as printing house from where a great amount of blocks had been cut and books that were called The Imperial Edition had been printed for the emperor.

From *Qianqingmen* (Gate of Heavenly Purity) to the north, is the inner court area. Located along the main axis is *Qianqinggong* (Palace of Heavenly Purity), *Jiaotaidian* (Hall of Union), *Kunninggong* (Palace of Earthly Tranquility) and the Imperial Garden. To the east of the middle route are the 6 east palaces for the emperor's concubines, *Yuqinggong* (Palace for the Crown Prince), *Fengxiandian* (Hall of Worshipping Ancestors) and *Zhaigong* (Palace of Abstinence), and to the west are the 6 west courtyards of palaces and *Yangxindian* (Hall of Mental Cultivation). Further to the east and west, there are respectively *Ci'ninggong* (Palace of Compassion and Tranquility) and *Shoukanggong* (Palace of Longevity and Well-Being), and *Ningshougong* (Palace of Tranquility and Longevity) precinct. The inner court area was built for the emperors' routine life and for the living and daily activities of the empress, the imperial concubines, princes and princesses.

Qianqinggong, *Jiaotaidian* and *Kunninggong* are regarded as a unity and are called as the 3 rear palaces. These three Palaces were the residential halls for the emperors and empresses in Ming dynasty, emperors in *Qianqinggong* which represents the hall of heaven, while the empresses in *Kunninggong* which means the hall of the earth. There are 12 courtyards of palaces for the imperial concubines at both sides of the 3 rear palaces, which were allotted to the high-ranking figures, and where the inferior ones had to occupy the side buildings. The Palace of Abstinence was used as the prelude of sacrificing and memorizing in the ancestral hall where tablets with names of the holy imperial pedigree were enshrined. Consecration always took place before important ceremonies, and in most cases, the emperor would be the role himself. An area in the northeast of Forbidden City was reconstructed into *Ningshougong* precinct, a set of palaces for the retired lives, when emperor Qianlong decided to abdicate in order not to reign longer than his grandfather who died after 61 year's rein. The spatial sequence imitated that of the imperial palace, which placed a frontcourt area and a rear abode area along a main axis and includes many palace buildings of names expecting longevity. But in fact, Emperor Qianlong never spent one night in the precinct.

Since Yongzheng period, there lived 8 emperors in *Yangxindian* (Hall of Mental Cultivation). The front hall of the court was for the ruler to deal with state affairs, and the rear hall was for residing. As *Ci'ninggong* (Palace of Compassion and Tranquility) and *Shoukanggong* (Palace of Longevity and Well-Being) were the palaces for the late emperor's consorts, they are also called courtyards for the widows.

3. The Building of *Wumen* and its Functions

Wumen (Meridian Gate) is the front portal of the Forbidden City, leading a series of gates in the city along the middle axis that ends with the north gate, *Shenwumen* (Gate of Martial Spirit). *Wumen* is named after the Chinese character standing for the south direction of meridian. The pier-like base of *Wumen* is U-shaped, 12 meters in height. This is the supreme form that is originated form the gateway plus watchtower model in archaic time. *Wumen* complex include a main building, four corner buildings and 13-bay-long corridors connecting the buildings, all covered with yellow glazed tiles. The main building has a decastyle facade and hexastyle side elevation. The four corner buildings and corridors stretch and embrace forward like wings. The four corner buildings and the main building are decorated with double-eaved roofs and forming an exquisite contour. This complex was entitled Five-Phoenix Building.

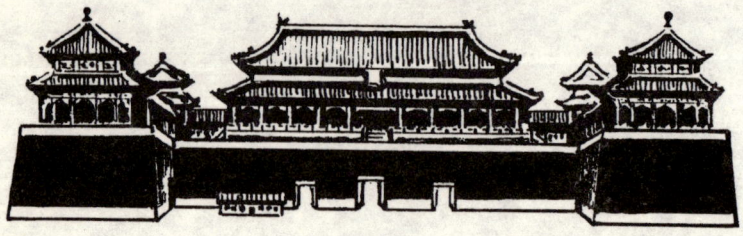

There are three front entrances on the facade, two on the wings facing west and east respectively, while on the north elevation all the 5 tunnels appear. It was the rule of Qing court that the middle tunnel was for the emperor, except that the empress may enter here once during the grand wedding ceremony and the 3 leading figures in imperial examinations may exit once after the Palace Examination. Ordinarily the civil and military officials enter from the east side entrance, while the nobility from the west one. Tunnels on the wings are closed until ceremonies are held in the Hall of Great Harmony or Palace Examination opens. The ways of entering are carefully stipulated. Before ceremonies, civil officials enter from the east entrance on the wing and the military from the west; before the examinations, candidates in odd numbers enter from the east wing tunnel and that in even numbers from the west.

A throne used to be placed in the main hall of the Five-Phoenix Building, and drum and bell in corner towers. The grand sight still can be recalled that in a sublime atmosphere, emperors arrived at ceremonies accompanied by bells and drums, and matched out for sacrificing events accompanied by bells.

After victory or conquer, the emperor should personally attend the ceremony at *Wumen* (Meridian Gate) and accept the surrenders. In Ming dynasty, lanterns were to be hung and banquets were to be held at *Wumen* on the 15th of the first month of the New Year according to lunar calendar. It was the time when ordinary people were allowed to come close and see the sight.

It should not be missed that the *Wumen* was also the place for so called Court Punishment.

4. The Corner Tower of the Imperial Palace

With its unique structure and splendid appearance, the Corner Tower is considered the most symbolic building in the Imperial Palace, which appears like bright attractive pearl inlaid at each of the four corners of the Forbidden City respectively.

The Corner Tower belonged to the defensive buildings in ancient times. Meanwhile, it also reflects the designers' intention to produce a paradise like result with artistic values. So its main function is for decorative purpose rather than practical one. It has no thick walls and observation openings, nor stories inside of the Tower. With its multi-eagles, ornaments and roof ridges, it looks ingenious and delicate. When you take a view of it from afar, you can find that the towering building rising from the level of the city wall, making it a unified entity completely. Its beautiful outlines intertwined with splendid painted beams and laths are reflected in the light green water, from which you can catch sight of a mysterious wonderful world.

The Corner Tower was originally built in the Ming Dynasty and renovated many times afterward. In 1957, the towers were repaired again. It was not until 1985 that the huge project was completely finished.

With a heavy and complicated structure, the Corner Tower

has a triple-eave roof composed with 27 flying-eave-corners, 10 decorated gablets, 72 hips and 230 zoomorphic ornaments that is more than twice the number of that on the roof of Hall of Great Harmony. According to the design requirements, no columns should be found to stand in the tower and not a single beam-end should be allowed to stretch out of the eave-corner as well. Complicated structure and demanding standards made the designers get nowhere. A legend goes, just when designers were at their wits end, Lu Ban, the master carpenter, deeply moved by their unremitting efforts and their indomitable spirit, descended to the world from the heaven one day with a katydid cage in his hand. The craftsmen made out at first glance that the katydid cage was just the very model of the corner tower they needed. They were overjoyed, but before they recognized who this person was Lu Ban had disappeared. Then they built the Corner Tower to the likeness of the katydid cage. It's indeed only a story, but it shows how elegant and complex the Tower really is and why it is so loved by people.

5. The Court Punishment at *Wumen*

As actor's line goes, the emperor demanded somebody "head-off outside *Wumen* (Meridian Gate)". It is so popular but not likely the truth except that the so called Court Punishment was executed at *Wumen*. Court Punishment is a special kind of punishment of beating some officials with staffs in Ming dynasty when they offended the emperor by going against the will of the ruler.

At the beginning of Emperor Zhu Yuanzhang's reign in early Ming dynasty, punishment in court was nothing more than a lashing or kneeling penalty, but in his late years, he had decapitated many. His son who reined the empire an even tougher hand had established astonishingly brutal tortures, such as peeling off skin, frying alive in deep oil, and dismembering the body. Court Punishment of staff beating came into being in *Chenghua* period (1465 – 1487).

Being taken by the imperial guards and brought to the *Wumen* and beaten on the back of the offender was the usual way. The exact place was east to the imperial road of the square. The 2 small houses at the foot of the base of *Wumen* were duty rooms for the guards. During execution, military officials were standing at the side halls (now the ticket offices) in the square. The offender was bound at the wrist wrapped in cloth. After being forced to lie prone, he would endure the punishment step by step. First, hearing the command of preparing staff, a guard would put the staff on his back, and after hearing the beating command, it should launch 3 times. If a command "beating hard" was heard, the punishment would continue. The beaters were to change every 5 beatings, and every beating was accompanied by shouting of all the guards. At last, 4 guards would grasp corners of the wrapping cloth and lift and throw the offender onto the ground. No doubt 8 or 9 of every 10 offenders died after the terrifying punishment.

6. Holding Court at Imperial Gate

"Yu Men Ting Zheng" (Listening to the Reports from Ministers at the Imperial Gate) was a significant way for the emperors to fulfill and demonstrate his diligent reign. As recorded in history, Emperor Liu Xun of West Han dynasty (reined from 73 to 49 BC) administered state affairs every 5 days. Much more impressively, Emperor Liu Xiu of East Han dynasty (reined from 25 to 57 AD) held court every day, and the famous emperor of Tang dynasty Li Shimin also personally dealt with state affairs frequently. Emperors of Ming and Qing dynasties continued to hold 2 traditional court affairs,i. e. Formal Audience and Listening to the Reports at the Imperial Gate.

Formal Audience and Listening to the Reports at the Imperial Gate were arranged simultaneous at *Fengtian Gate* (*Taihemen* in Qing dynasty) in Ming dynasty, and together were called "Chang Chao Yu Men Yi" (Formal Audience and Performing Royal Rites at Imperial Gate). Beginning with drums on *Wumen* (Meridian Gate), the rite required ministers to organize outside the gate tunnel and not walk in until the bell rang. Officials should follow the sequence and the division of civil and military to enter through the wing tunnels at both sides and pass the inner golden river to reach *Taihemen* (Gate of Great Harmony). Lead by the princes and dukes, everyone must stand in his position according to the rank along both sides of the road to the stairs. The emperor appearing, whips were to be lashed resonantly, and officials should kneel down to pay respect to the emperor and present memorial in order. In secret cases, reports were usually made after the others. After all the presentations, whips re-lashed, the emperor left and then the ministers moved out in sequence.

Rites were so extremely strict in Ming dynasty that uproarious talk, murmuring, coughing or spitting were deemed as violating the rites, let alone trespass the queues. Presenters should detour from the end of each queue to the front of the emperor, and kneel down while speaking, and return the same way afterwards. Even tiny violations would be investigated by inspectors and brought to the emperor for punishment.

"Chang Chao Yu Men Yi" frequently took place during early Ming dynasty, and Emperor Jingtai even called for noon court. But after Jiajing period, maybe owing to the incident of some inner court maids' murder attempt, holding court at the imperial gate was gradually fade out from emperors' minds, and in the seldom cases, ministers also forgot their position in the queues and even debated seriously.

The rites and rules were inherited by the Qing dynasty, but not the place. Formal Audience was held at the *Taihemen* (Gate of Great Harmony), while "Listening to the Reports from Ministers at the Imperial Gate" took place at *Qianqingmen*, the Gate of Heavenly Purity that leads to the rear abode area.

In Qing dynasty, "Yu Men Ting Zheng" was summoned by the emperor when memorials to the throne totaled up to a certain amount, and the date was to be carefully chosen. The Grand Secretariat was the first to know the command, and in turn informed the ministers to prepare for the folds. When the time came, a set of furniture including a throne, a table, a back screen and a felt pad for the presenter was placed in the middle bay of the gate hall. The officials of ministries gathered at rest rooms and then waited outside the Middle Left Gate for the emperor's order to attend the court in front of *Qianqingmen*. After everyone took his position, the emperor arrived by sedan chair from the interior. The official recorder mounted the platform of *Qianqingmen* and stood by the west column, one by one the ministers should kneel down on the pad and present the contents of his memorial to the throne and return to the original position afterwards. Usually, there should also be a secretary minister who placed a report container on the table, so that the emperor received and replied to each presentation. After the presentation was completed, the emperor departed, and then the ministers followed.

When the emperor was on trips, "Yu Men Ting Zheng" should also be held at temporary dwellings. Emperor Kangxi is the most diligent of all who kept the regulation every day. It is not surprising that many of the important historical decisions were made at the gate.

In general, Holding Court at the Gate was of greatest importance in the thoughts of all the emperors, for it demonstrates his sympathy to the people and his diligence. The place could be alternative in bad weather. Kindness and gifts were always distributed during gate court, but it never meant that disciplines for the participating officials were not strict. As the old saying goes, Court at Gate, Rite at Stake, it was recorded that Emperors Qianlong and Daoguang had the late and absent de-ranked and fined.

7. Architectural Characteristics of the Three Front Halls

Symbolizing the Imperial power, the 3 front halls are of the most sublime status in the Forbidden City. The halls are located on the triple platform that is surrounded with carved balustrades. *Taihedian* (Hall of Great Harmony) is in the front of the three, and followed by *Zhonghedian* (Hall of Middle Harmony) and *Baohedian* (Hall of Preserving Harmony). The plan platform shapes a Chinese character "土" meaning earth that occupies the center of the land in traditional believing. Grandeurs and dignified as the complex is, it arouses the feeling that the buildings were heaven palaces built on the earth.

The three front halls were originally built in 1420 during Emperor Yongle's reign and had undergone many rebuilds and

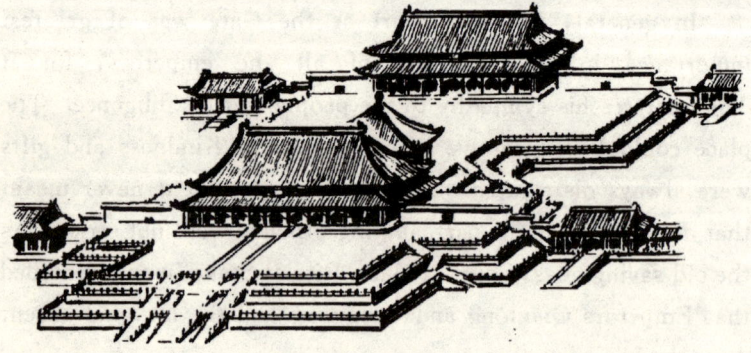

repairs. The complex is the heart of the Forbidden City and that of the city of Beijing. All the grandest ceremonies were held here during Ming and Qing dynasties, and the scale, style and details were designed to adopt highest level. *Taihedian* is most representative among them.

The building of *Taihedian* had a facade of 11 bays, and a 5-bay side elevation. It is unique in existing historical buildings in China that the hall covers 2,300 square meters. The height is 35.5 meters, and the roof style is called Wu-dian that is the highest level of all traditional styles, and is forbidden to use in residential buildings of ordinary people. The style of the triple white stone platform is called *Xumizuo* (Sumaru Base), which is delicately carved and decorated with dragon and phoenix balusters and balustrades. The grand carved path of dragon and clouds patterns in the middle of the stairs was for the emperor only. Tile decorations on the corner ridges of the eaves are also different from that of the other buildings which are usually composed of figures of odd numbers not more than 9, but here on *Taihedian* (Hall of Great Harmony), it can be seen that 10 figures are used to identify the special status of the building.

Inside the Hall of Great Harmony, the ground is paved with so called "gold" bricks, and a 1-meter-high platform is placed in the center of hall. The supreme throne, lacquered and carved with dragon motif, is on the platform, accompanied by incense table and incense burner on both sides in the front and a screen lacquered and carved with dragon motif behind. Threateningly and majestically, 6 gilt dragon coiled pillars in 2 rows and a dragon caisson ceiling on the top are architectural vocabularies applied to emphasize the throne. On the platform in front of the hall are a bronze tortoise and a bronze crane that stand for longevity, and a holy sundial and a standard measurer that tells the power of the emperor's control of both time and space. During ceremonies, incenses and pine branches were burnt in bronze crane, tortoise and burners. Heavenly palaces floated on clouds, *Taihedian* is situated sedately behind the coiling incense smoke, together with the coiling ode, as long as sky and earth exist, the state prospers.

Since the three front halls were built for different functions, building styles were not the same, but were coordinated with each other into a unity. *Taihedian* has a grandeur and sublime facade, *Baohedian* is simpler but sedate, and *Zhonghedian* is square in shape and smaller and links the other 2 halls. The complex of 3 halls and building enclosures reflects the most outstanding characteristic of Chinese architectural achievements and the ancient design philosophy.

8. Grand Ceremony at *Taihedian*

Taihedian, the Hall of Great Harmony, symbolizes the power of emperor. Following Ming convention, Qing emperors held grand ceremonies, such as enthroning, wedding, titling the empress, celebrating the emperor's birthday, lunar New Year's Day and the Winter Solstice at *Taihedian*. Ceremony for mounting the throne was the greatest of all when the emperor was to accept respect and congratulations of his ministers and diplomatic envoys who came to the empire. Procedures and rites of the ceremony are also representative.

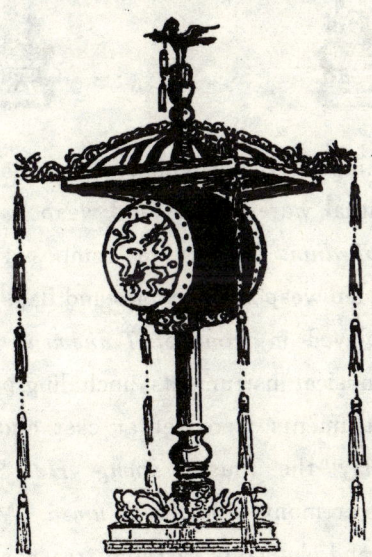

The date of the ceremony should be chosen and settled by Imperial Astronomy Office. All responding organizations were to prepare for the event after the notice, and the day right before, officials were sent to sacrifice to the Heaven, the Earth, ancestors and the God of Land and Harvest.

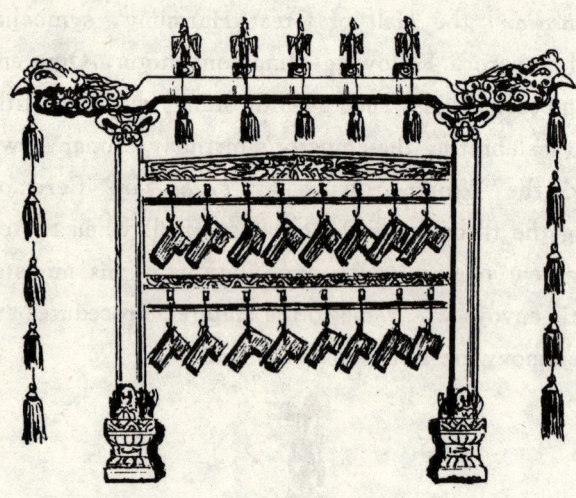

In the morning of the ceremony, imperial honor guards placed a set of ritual wares, flags and weapons along the road which lead to *Taihedian*. The set was composed of 500 gold and silver wares, wooden weapons, canopies and flags. Yellow dragon canopy was displayed in front of *Taihemen* (Gate of Great Harmony), and musical instruments, including percussion, wind and stringed instruments were set at east and west sides of *Taihedian* to play the music *Zhong He Shao Yue* that accompanied the ceremony. Outside *Wumen* (Meridian Gate), stood 5 cart sets and elephants carrying treasure vases. All the princes, dukes, and officials should be in court robes, with official hat and court beads on. On the occasion, hearing the first drum, all attendees in queue would wait outside Meridian Gate, and after the second drum, follow rite conductors in. When music was played, the emperor in dragon robe left the rear palace by sedan chair. The first stop was the Hall of Middle Harmony. Accepting respects and congratulations of his entourage, the emperor might have a rest and preparation for the grand ceremony. After everything was settled, the sovereign mounted the throne in the music of *Zhong He Shao Yue* in *Taihedian* (Hall of Great Harmony). Whips were lashed resonantly three times, telling officials military and civil to stand in their positions. Then an announcer read congratulation speeches loudly, and all officials knelt and kowtowed to the new ruler, yelling Long Live Your Majesty! Finally, the ceremony ended after the emperor returned to the rear palace and the officials disassembled. Later on, one great scholar would carry an imperial edict with the imperial seal out from *Wumen* (Meridian Gate) to *Tian'anmen* (Gate of Heavenly Peace). The imperial edict was read by an honor guard

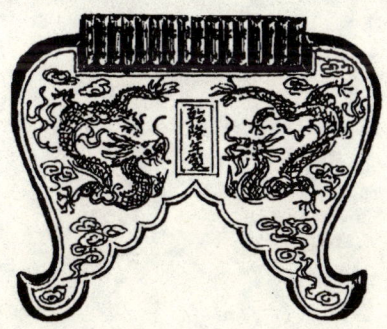

and a commander, and then transported down the wall base by descending a golden phoenix holding the edict in the mouth. This is the most popular saying of Imperial Edict in Phoenix Beak.

It should be noted that during the ceremony, heavenly palaces floated on clouds of incense, *Taihedian* was situated sedately behind the coiling smoke, together with the coiling ode, as long as sky and earth exist, the state prospers.

Sometimes after the ceremony, banquets were to be given to the officials. Anyway, it can be imagined that for many aged ministers, after waiting and standing, and being afraid of violating rites all the time from dawn, no food could be as delicious as it should be.

9. Publicizing Imperial Edict

Since ancient times, the emperor had been always regarded as the son of the Heaven, and his power was believed to be given by the Heaven. So emperor's command was the will of Heaven. Imperial edicts would not be publicized unless grand rites were held.

Edicts were given to the world whenever great events took place, when the emperor mounted the throne, married or was going to send expeditions.

Publicizing imperial edict was an extremely important event in the court, and the designated place was *Taihedian* (Hall of Great Harmony). The Board of Rite, the Board of Works and the Imperial Procession Guard should carefully prepare for the ceremony in advance. A yellow table should be placed in the middle of the Hall of Great Harmony, and another in the center of the platform. Honor props including an imperial canopy and a tray with cloud pattern were also to be displayed here, while at *Wumen* (Meridian Gate), officials from the Board of Works would prepare a gold phoenix for the event. When the ceremony began, an academician of the Grand Secretariat would respectfully hold out the imperial edict, and then place it in the tray on the yellow table. After a while, the emperor would mount the throne and receive respects of the ministers. The next step was that the grand academician took the edict to the official from the Board of Rite under the eave of *Taihedian*, and the later knelt down and kowtowed to receive, and turn it into the hands of another official from the same ministry. The receiver escorted by the honor guards matched out from *Taihemen* (Gate of Great Harmony) and *Wumen* (Meridian Gate), and put the edict in a dragon pavilion. In the ceremonial music, the pavilion would be carried by the honor guards to *Tian'anmen* that was the front gate of the imperial city, and had always been regarded as the most important place for the empire. Right in the center of the building of *Tian'anmen* the pavilion would be placed. Next came the announcer who would take the edict out from the pavilion, put it onto another yellow table, and then read it. Officials civil and military were to kneel down to listen to the announcement which would be read twice in Mandarin and the language of Manchu. Finally an edict receiver would hand and bind it at the beak of the gold phoenix. Dropped down from the middle of the wall base, the edict was to be replaced into the dragon pavilion and transported from the *Daqingmen* (Gate of Great Qing) to the office building of the Board of Rite where a yellow table and incense burners were prepared to respectfully receive it. The imperial edict would be printed and publicized all over the country.

In the following stories, with no exceptions local officials of provincial or county level would kneel down to receive the edict, and when passing by the promulgating troop, all the people must prostrate at right side of the road. Such ceremony with props of dragon pavilion and flags had to be repeated from high governmental branches to the lower, till the edict was publicized to all.

10. Story of the Throne in Taihedian

You must have been attracted by the carved lacquer throne with dragon patterns located aloft on the platform in the center of *Taihedian* (Hall of Great Harmony). Its style and decorative patterns are unique, and it is perfectly accompanied with interior settings and architectural vocabularies. It was the most important and symbolic throne of the emperors and quite different from the imperial seats placed in the other halls in the Forbidden City. The throne is elegantly shaped and delicately carved. The back and arm rails are composed of 3 coiling dragons, and the backboard is also decorated with dragon design.

The seating base of the throne adopted a traditional Sumeru base. All the surface of the seating is covered with gold foil. There is a Sumeru-shaped foot-rest in front of the throne and a lacquered and gilt screen behind the seat. As the most symbolic vocabulary, only gold and dragon are used to accompany the emperor. Incense burners in the shapes of elephant, *Luduan*, crane, tube and vessel had given off coiling smoke to dignify the emperors, the hall and the power of the empire for centuries.

Is the throne original? Which emperor was the owner? Here is a story to tell.

In 1915 when a warlord Yuan Shikai seized the highest power and intended to restore the dethroned emperor, he found the throne too high for him and asked to make a new one that mixed Chinese and western styles in it. In his special request, the seating board was lowered down, and in the meantime the back was heightened to compensate for the whole scale and the shrunk dignity. History proved by no means such an imperial seat could possibly match the interior and settings of the Hall of Great Harmony, but searching efforts for the original failed in 1947 when the Palace Museum formally handed over the possession of the Museum of Antiquities. All they found were nothing but lacquered dragon seats that did not belong to the supreme set, either in different scale or in different style. The problem was not solved until in 1959 when Mr. Zhu Jiajin, a famous historian of the Imperial Court of the Palace Museum noticed an old photo taken in 1900 (the 26th year of Emperor Guangxu's reign in Qing dynasty) that tells original interior settings and furniture styles. Basing on this clue, Mr. Zhu aided by other experts at last found a dilapidated seat in a warehouse for damaged furniture. In depth research showed that work methodology of lacquer and the carving of the seat is in accordance with that of Ming dynasty, and most likely it is the one that made when *Taihedian* was rebuilt in Jiajing period of Ming. By the evidence that a portrait of Emperor Kangxi has the exact the same throne as a prop, it is also believed that though there had been many repairs and rebuilds, especially the greatest one in Kangxi period in Qing dynasty, the throne had not been deserted. Having accompanied so many emperors young or old, tall or short, the throne was not consigned to limbo until Yuan Shikai usurped the state power.

In 1963, the throne was carefully restored according to historical records. Virtuosi and top craftsmen were selected, and a year's time and a total of 934 labor days were used before the restoration was completed in September of 1964. Escorted by interior surroundings, the throne shines again in the brilliant hall.

11. Furnishings and Implications in Front of the Throne in *Taihedian*

Inside the resplendent and magnificent *Taihedian* (Hall of Great Harmony), furnishings in pairs are placed in front of the dragon throne. They are 2 elephants, 2 *Luduan*, 2 cranes, 2 incense tubes and 4 incense burners.

Whenever the emperor appeared, incense of sandalwood would be burned in these furnishings, making an even more mys terious and solemn atmosphere. There are also stories of the furnishings, either of the spirit creatures or of the ancient wares,

which are respected and used for the meaning of felicity, longevity, stability and prosperity.

The spirit elephant is thought of as the Peace Carrier. The pair displayed in *Taihedian* (Hall of Great Harmony) is made of copper-bodied enamel. The Peace is symbolized by the grand vase placed on the back of the elephant, for they bear the same pronunciation in Chinese, while the elephant has another meaning of "the scene", strong and docile stands for stability of the state. So together the peace carrier represents the auspicious scene of the peaceful state. Moreover, five cereals or other propitious artifacts are usually put in the vase to pray for a good harvest. Bringing peace and prosperity to the empire and plentiful life to the people, the elephant is most frequently used to decorate the emperor's side.

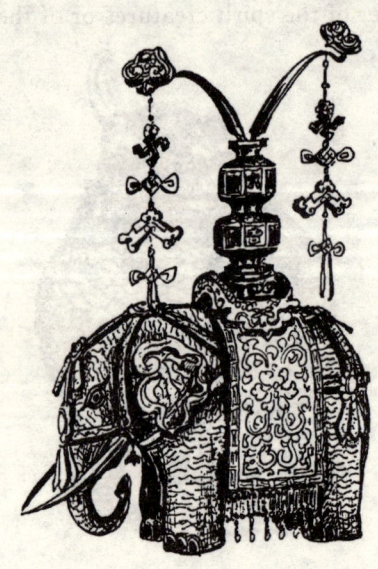

Luduan is a legendary animal that knows many languages of places near and afar. It can also run 18,000 *li* (9,000 km) in one day, so it does not only bring knowledge from every corner of the world, but also guards and serves the emperor with the omni book, showing the lord's justice and awareness of every single detail. The pair in front of the supreme throne is also made of copper-bodied enamel.

The crane that is believed to have the power of bringing the dying back to life is a spirit bird in ancient Chinese tales. She is the incarnation of youthful longevity. No doubt cranes are placed here for the best wishes of the health of the emperor and the everlasting reign of him and his offspring.

Incense burners here in *Taihedian* are made of cloisonné enamel in Qianlong period imitating the ancient ritual vessel *Ding*. Lotus flowers linked with branches and tendrils are depicted all over, and elephant heads are used as the triple feet of the pot. Shining with primitive simplicity, the incense pot has a long history of being displayed in the imperial court as a prop for praying to the Heaven and a propitious ware as well.

The incense tube is another style of the incense burner used to furnish the imperial palaces. The tube in *Taihedian* is also made of cloisonné enamel. Because it has a pavilion like cover on the top, the incense tube is also called as incense pavilion. The body of the tube is hollowed out with coiling dragon patterns so that smoke can come out from the openworked holes. The tube stands for peace, stability and unity of the empire.

12. "Gold" Brick Pavement

The saying spreads widely in the country that palaces of the emperor are so luxurious that the ground is paved with gold. It is equally eloquent that the pavement inside *Taihedian* shines so brilliantly with such tenderness, fineness and smoothness, and above all it comforts the foot as well as the eye. Having no cement and modern building technology, the pavement survived changes of 500 years and is still kept its perfect performance. What a miracle! This kind of pavement is so-called gold ground, using a special kind of "gold" bricks made of clay.

"Gold" bricks were made exclusively for the imperial palaces. Suzhou was the major area that produced "gold" bricks, because of its fine and glutinous clay and its convenient location near the Grand Canal that directly leads to the capital.

The working methods of making "gold" bricks are unique

and complicated. The first step is finding suitable clay. The requirement includes cohesiveness and fineness. It should cohere well and contain no sand. The following step is to soak the clay in water, and in the meanwhile step on it to make putty. And then temper it repeatedly, which is called taming the clay. Put the tamed clay into the mould and press the mould on the top with the weight of 2 men to make the clay condensed and tight. After dried in the shade, the molded clay is to be baked in kilns. It is recorded that the baking should be 130-days long divided into 4 steps, first fired with weeds, then with small firewood, then firewood, and at last with pine branches. Each piece of brick would be examined after baking, and only those that sounded well when knocked and no tiny holes that could be detected when split could pass. Paving is quite an art as well. All the bricks are to be grinded to joint each other at extreme tightness. It is called *Mo Zhuan Dui Feng*, which is to make the pavement jointless. We still can read in the building norms of Qing dynasty that 1 laborer could only cut and grind 3 pieces of bricks that is 2 *chi* (app. 64cm) square in 1 workday, and when paving, 1 brick layer with 2 unskilled laborers could only make 5 pieces in 1 workday. Finally, dye material and Tong oil is to be poured onto the surface and to be polished with melted wax to complete the process.

There are altogether 4,718 pieces of "gold" bricks paved inside the Hall of Great Harmony. Though it is not gold, is it inferior to gold? "Gold" brick is a laudatory title, and it deserves.

13. No Trees in the Outer Court

Although summer gives the visitors and had given the emperors the same scorching sun, from *Taihemen* (Gate of Great Harmony) to the 3 front halls and then to the square before *Qianqingmen* (Gate of Heavenly Purity), in the spaces along more than a half of the main axis in the city no tree can be found. Why?

The question can be explicated when the architectural layout and functions of the Forbidden City are taken into consideration. As we know, the Forbidden City is divided into the front court area and the back abode area at the square in front of *Qianqingmen*. The 3 front halls, *Taihedian*, *Zhonghedian* and *Baohedian*, are the central part of the front court area and was the

place for the emperors to hold grand ceremonies. In the rear abode area, there are 12 palaces for the empress and concubines located at both sides of the 3 rear palaces in the middle. The rear part is more compactly arranged and of richer flavor of life than the front part.

Since the front area is mainly built for grand ceremonies, spatial arrangement and building styles all reflect characteristics of symbolizing dignity of the emperor and the absolute imperial power. Placing the 3 front halls on a 7-meter-high triple platform itself cannot show more clearer that the chief role is the hall, and no disturbing factors natural nor manmade would be allowed. Giant old trees can bring sublime atmosphere in mausoleums or gardens, but not here in the sole space of the sovereign.

Another reason for the bare square might be that the tree would be in the way when lines of honor guards and officials were assembled. Canopies, flags and weapon would be only better demonstrated in plainest space.

We can conclude that because of the functional reasons for the building trees were not planted in the front court area from *Wumen* (Meridian Gate) to *Qianqingmen* (Gate of Heavenly Purity). Actually, outside the Forbidden City there had been no trees from *Tian'anmen* (Gate of Heavenly Peace) to *Wumen* during Ming and Qing dynasties, the trees we see now between the gates were planted after the fall of Qing dynasty.

14. Sedan Chairs for Qing Emperors

It was the sedan chairs that carried the emperor and his empress and concubines in and out of the Forbidden City. There are many kinds of sedan chairs that have strict regulations of use for many different occasions. The royal court had a designated organization for controlling the sedans and a specific place for storing them. The organization was called *Luanyiwei*, the Imperial Procession Guard, subordinate to Imperial Household Department, and the storage was called *Luanjiaku*, the storage for honor props, located to the south of the east gate inside the Forbidden City.

Sedans are called *Yu* in Mandarin. According to the Rites, *Yu* for the emperor's different usages varied, some were for ceremonies, and some were for going on inspection outside his palace. Taking going out for example, there used to be *Li Yu* (*Yu* for the Rites), *Bu Yu* (*Yu* for the pace), *Qing Bu Yu* (*Yu* for the light pace), *Bian Yu* (sedan for convenience) and etc. What's more, lines of honor props were to be demonstrated before the sedans, which have the special names as *Da Jia*, *Fa Jia*, *Luan Jia* and *Qi Jia*. Empress dowager, empress and imperial concubines of different ranks had their own honor guards and furnishings, including *Yu* of dragon and phoenix, *Yu* of phoenix, *Yu* of spirit bird and simple *Yu*. After wedding ceremony, the royal couple would use a special phoenix *Yu* decorated with patterns of double happiness. Now let us have a closer look at sedans for the emperor.

Li Yu, *Yu* for the Rites is the highest grade sedan that the emperor used in grand ceremonies inside or outside the Forbidden City, such as Court Ceremony at *Taihedian* (Hall of Great Harmony), consecration ceremonies at the Temple of Heaven or at Ancestral Temple. *Yu* for the Rites is the most respected, most sublimely and gorgeously decorated sedan. Its appearance is basically similar with that used by ordinary people, but far larger in size and far delicately decorated. It has 14 bars for 16 carriers to shoulder. The curtains are made of yellow satin. There are 2 canopies covering on the top, the upper in octagon, the lower in square. In the middle of the canopies is the golden vault of the sedan room. The room has 2 windows on both sides that use glass sheets in winter and blue gauze in summer. The imperial dragon seat is placed inside. There used to be more than 1,500 honor guards holding honor furnishings matching in front of the emperor.

Bu Yu, *Yu* for the pace took the emperor anywhere inside the imperial city. It looks like a folk mountain sedan, or an imperial seat with bars at both sides. It is wooden with a gilt lacquer finish and carved dragon patterns. There would be sable fur cushion in winter and yellow satin cushion in summer. A foot rest is fixed in front of the seat, also decorated with dragon and cloud patterns. There are 14 main bars and branches altogether for 16 carriers. *Yu* for the pace is lead by a band and an honor guard troop of about 100 men and escorted with a troop of bodyguards.

Qing Bu Yu, *Yu* for the light pace was used when the emperor would go on inspections or hunting outside the imperial city. It was smaller than the *Yu* for the pace and was carried by 16 men. Band and troops surrounded the sedan totally up to 200-300 people.

Apart from the above-mentioned sedans, the emperor also has a kind of *Bianyu*, *Yu* for using at will. It was used daily inside the Forbidden City, and it is even small in size for 4 or 8 men to shoulder. People escorting this kind of sedan are far less in number.

The sedans displayed in *Zhonghedian* (Hall of Middle Harmony) are both *Bian Yu*. We have no examples of other kinds, except that which can be seen in historical paintings. One of the famous paintings is the *Banquet in Garden of Tens of Thousands Trees*. Emperor Qianlong is in a *Qing Bu Yu*.

Bands to accompany the imperial sedans are indispensable

and are various according to different grades. Carriers were chosen by the Imperial Household Department. They all should be in red satin. Eunuchs were used to carry sedans when the emperor traveled in the palaces or imperial gardens. The south room in the west row of *Qianqinggong* (Palace of Heavenly Purity) had been the place for sedan serving department. There used to be more than 30 eunuchs waiting for command. The department has a mandarin name, Shang Cheng Jiao.

15. Palace Examination of Qing Dynasty

The Palace Examination is the highest-level test in Imperial Examination System for selecting officials. The system was established in Tang dynasty during the Empress Wu Zetian's reign, and was followed ever since. Imperial Examination of Qing dynasty has four levels, i. e. *Tongshi* (Basic level), *Xiangshi* (provincial examination), *Huishi* (joint examination) and *Dianshi* (Palace Examination). *Tongshi* covers examination in counties and municipalities, learners would be called as *Xiucai* after passing the basic level exam. *Xiucai* might attend the next trial every 3 years in the provincial capitals to gain a Juren degree. Further, Juren could take part into the examinations hosted by the Board of Rites in Beijing once every 3 years. The winners would have the title of *Gongshi*. Only *Gongshi* were allowed to appear in the final examination in the palace which was chaired and invigilated by the emperor himself. Those selected after answering to the emperor's question would receive highest rank of scholars, *Jinshi*.

The Palace Examinations of Qing dynasty started in the 3rd year of Shunzhi period (1646). At the early years of Qing, the examination place had been designated outside *Tian'anmen* (Gate of Heavenly Peace), and later had also changed to the open space in front of *Taihedian* (Hall of Great Harmony) in 1658. In the first year of Emperor Yongzheng's reign, he ordered to use the interior space of *Taihedian* because of the cold weather. The rule was set finally by Emperor Qianlong who used *Baohedian* (Hall of Preserving Harmony) as the examination hall.

Questions in palace examinations were all assigned by the emperor. After the examiners raised the questions, then the emperor decided which ones were to be used in the exam. And then the questions would be printed secretly the night before the exam. All the procedures were safely guarded and strictly inspected. After the examinees finished their papers, officials  were to evaluate and mark them repeatedly. The names, curriculum vitae and family background of the first 10 papers were concealed for emperor's decision. The decision of the positions of the names would be written on 2 announcements; the smaller one was for the emperor's inspection, and the great announcement was to be publicized outside *Chang'anzuomen* (Chang'anzuo Gate), and be announced in the ceremony at *Taihedian*. The event was imposing and solemn.

The first 30 successful examinees used to be classified into 3 categories, and the leading 3 of the first 10 were conferred respectively the titles of Zhuangyuan, Bangyan and Tanhua, and would be assigned to be members of Hanlin Academy.

16. Story of the Grand Stone Carving behind *Baohedian*

There is a giant piece of stone carving with patterns of dragon, cloud, sea waves and mountains in the middle of the imperial stairs behind *Baohedian* (Hall of Preserving Harmony). Stones at the same location of the stairs are called the imperial path where nobody else was allowed to walk on. This giant piece was originally carved in Ming dynasty when the 3 front halls were erected. In the 25th year of Emperor Qianlong's reign, Ming works were removed and carvings were redone. It is what we see today, 9 dragons coiling in and out of the clouds over the curling waves and mountains at the bottom with rim pattern of interlacing lotus. The fine works is not only famous for its carving but also for its great size that is 16.67 meters long, 3.07 meters wide and 1.70 meters thick. The stone came from Fangshan County in the west suburbs of Beijing. Experts estimated that the material stone weighed at least 300 tons. It has been frequently asked how the stone was transported and why it had not been placed at the most important location in front of *Taihedian* (Hall of Great harmony).

The legend says that Ming workers poured water on the road in winter to make ice and used the method to move a special ship along the ground to transport the stone to the palace. Wells

were dug every *li* (a half kilometer), and 10,000 labors were employed to complete in 1 month. We cannot tell the exact date or year, but it was inferred that the time was before building the Forbidden City; otherwise it is impossible to pass the gates after gates.

As for its location, it might be beyond the imagination of architects at that time. The reason is supposed to be that the stone was transported to the place where it is now and then carved but not possible to move anymore. Accidentally, it might prove that the stone carving is older than the Forbidden City, that is, more than 580 years old.

17. Tile Decoration on the Roofs
in the Forbidden City

On the various kinds of ridges on roofs in the Forbidden City, many decorative tile works in shapes of animals can be found. The most noticeable figure is the one at the two ends of the main ridge, *Wen*, or giant *Wen*, one of the nine sons of the dragon; the smaller ones include decorative components in rows at slope ridges, hip ridges and corner ridges. These glazing tile works are indispensable on the buildings in the Forbidden City and other formal architectural settings at that time.

The pair of *Wen* at the both ends of the main ridge on the roof of *Taihedian*, the largest of all existing tile works in China, is a composition of 13 individual pieces of glazed tile components.

Each *Wen* is 340 cm high, 268 cm wide and 32cm thick, and weighs 4. 3 tons. It has delicate dragon patterns with a sword at the back showing only the handle. The legend says that *Wen* was punished to stay on the roof to prevent buildings from fire for the guilt committed, and the sword and shackles are used to bind it in place. More actual than tales and propitious wishes, *Wen* marks a beautiful skyline for the great halls, and supply further waterproof at the weak point on the joints of ridges as well.

Lead by the decoration of a Spirit riding on a cock, Animal figures on eave corners also vividly carved and glazed. The application of these decorations differs in numbers according to the status of building. The only supreme example is *Taihedian* that has 10 on each corner ridge, and that of other buildings varies from 9 to 1 in odd numbers. What ever is used, the sequence of the figure is fixed. We can count the ultimate 10 as an example, dragon, phoenix, lion, sky horse, sea horse, spirit lion, fish, spirit deer (unicorn), ox, and the tenth, a monkey. The row of decorations, the row of spirits from the Heaven, matching down on the flying eave as people call the curved roof contour of the building, each represents a story either auspicious or annihilating evil. Similar to the functions of *Wen*, the decorations have their own tasks as building components. They are applied at the joint line of 2 roof surfaces and at the ridge slope downwardly and fixed with stakes so that waterproof is enhanced and slippery of the ridge is prevented. Functional components taking on decorative and symbolical coat is a perfect as well as typical tendency of architectural evolution under the hands of designer generation after generation.

18. Imperial Palace—the Dragon's World

Many people have counted the stone lions of the Lugou Bridge but no one knows for sure how many dragons there are in the Forbidden City.

The Dragon, a mysterious animal in the Chinese myth legend, originates from the totem of a clan tribe in the ancient times. As a symbol of the Chinese nation, its appearance is being perfected along with the development of the history. We can roughly describe it as something with "ox-head, deer-horn, snake-body, fish-scales and eagle-claw".

Since the Han and Tang Dynasties, "dragon" was possessed exclusively by the ruling class, and thus became the symbol of

the Chinese emperor. The emperor always styled himself the son
of the real dragon. So, the Forbidden City—the emperors'
residence of the Ming and Qing Dynasties, is therefore closely
related to the "dragon". When strolling among the palaces, the
dragon image can be seen everywhere. For example, the Hall of
the Great Harmony, as a place of holding grand ceremonies in old
days, the décor of the dragon design was obtained full
embodiments. It is omnipresent whether on the gold-lacquer
painted throne and the screen surrounded behind it, or on the six
gilt pillars and ceilings. Furthermore, a vivid dragon is carved in
high relief on the cession at the center of the ceiling. In its mouth
is a Xuanyuan Mirror, which means that Chinese emperors as the
descendants of *Huang Di* (the Emperor Huang), were the sons
of the real dragon. The robe worn by the emperor in ceremony
always carried the dragon designs. Moreover, the dragon image

was also used on the furniture, ornamental settings, the utensils, such as the four treasures of the study (writing brush, ink stick, ink slab and paper), clocks, jade wares, lacquer wares, porcelains, etc. In addition, it was even decorated on food, instruments or some items used for marriage ceremony or obsequies and some other happy events or occasions.

Recently, the number of the dragon images decorated on the Hall of Great Harmony has been calculated. The details are as follows: on the roof embracing 5 ridges, end-tiles, and drip-tiles, are 2, 632 dragon designs, on the outer-eave gates and windows including their decors are painted with 5,  732 dragons; the inner-eave beams, purlins and ceilings have 4, 037 dragons, on the columns, caisson, and on the throne, screen and ornamental furnishings, are altogether 609 dragons; on the inside-walls, hanging partitions of the door, have 542 dragons. According to incomplete statistics, the Hall of Great Harmony alone has 13,800 dragons.

After painstaking efforts, perhaps one can count roughly the number of dragons in the Hall of Great Harmony, but the dragons in the whole Forbidden City may remain to be an unknown number forever.

19. Stories of Outdoor Imperial Furnishings

Large bronze or iron vats, bronze tortoises, bronze cranes, holy sundials and holy measure can be found in many places in the Forbidden City. All these are outdoor furnishings in the imperial palace.

Giant vats, especially the 10 in one row at both sides of *Qianqingmen* (Gate of Heavenly Purity) shining in the sunlight and accompanied with the plain red wall, had silently decorated and protected the Forbidden City for centuries. Protect? Yes, these vats had been full of clean water for emergencies in case of fire. During winter time, eunuchs from Imperial Household Department were responsible for coating the vats with cotton covers, capping them, and making fire at the bottom to prevent

freezing. After the fall of Qing dynasty, the vats had been neglected until when the Palace Museum was established and decided to drill holes at the bottom to let the collected water out.

Bronze and iron vats were made in Ming dynasty, while the gilt copper ones were Qing castings.

The tortoise and crane have been favorite creatures in China since ancient times. The tortoise represents longevity, and the crane stands for auspiciousness. That is the reason why spirit tortoise and crane are placed in front of many important buildings in the Forbidden City, symbolizing longevity and propitiousness for the emperor and prosperity of the empire. It is certain that the pair that furnishes *Taihedian* is the largest and the most exquisite of all. Stable as the tortoise, graceful as the crane, they balance perfectly visually as well as meaningfully.

The statue of bronze tortoise and crane both have a hollow body that opens in the mouth. There is also a movable cover on the shell or the back. When grand ceremonies were to be held, incense and pine branches were put in from the top cap, and smoke would come out from the mouth. Mysterious smoke coiling around the hall was thus produced.

Holy measure is the standard measurement in ancient China. One in cubic shape and one in round are separately placed in front of *Taihedian* and *Qianqinggong*. Both of them were made in the 9th year of the Qianlong period. Holy measure is a composition of 5 volume units, *Hu* on the top, *Dou* on the bottom, *Sheng* at left side, *Ge* at top of the right side and *Yue* at the bottom of it.

Holy sundials tell the time by the length and direction of the pointer. In ancient China, the first recorded invention and use can be traced back to Han dynasty (140 BC to 220 AD).

Furnishings of the holy measure and holy sundial lost its original function when emperor of Ming and Qing dynasties demanded to display them. They have been standing there for centuries manifesting that it is the emperor who provides the country measurement and chronometer, who controls the space and time, and who holds the supreme power.

20. Inner Golden River inside the Forbidden City

Golden River refers to the river of the Forbidden City. The outer part of the Golden River passes in front of *Tian'anmen* (Gate of Heavenly Peace), another part of it that serpentines inside the city is called Inner Golden River.

The Inner Golden River runs into the Forbidden City through the tunnel at the foot of the wall on northwest corner. It passes *Wuyingdian* (Hall of the Military Eminence), *Taihemen* (Gate of Great Harmony), and the courtyard between *Wenhuadian* (Hall of Literary Glory) and *Wenyuan'ge* (Pavilion of Source of Literature), heading southeast. After crossing the road that leads to the east gate of the city, the river goes out at the southeast corner into the city moat. The 2 km long Inner Golden River links the north and south part of the city moat.

The bottom and revetments of the Inner Golden water river are all built with white stone, and its width varies every now and then all the way. The curves and turns make it a flexible ribbon among the strict building complex.

Today there are tens of bridges across the river. The 5 stone arch bridges in front of *Taihemen* are the most delicate in carving and solemn in style of all. Seen from *Taihemen*, the Inner Golden River shapes a bow like curve, full of elasticity, and the white marble bridges are the giant arrows to be shot. The 5 elegant bridges are located at the most important path on the axis of the city. In the middle is the imperial path that is the widest and longest of the five. The other 4 bridges on both sides were for the noble and the officials, and were of inferior status to the main bridge. Carving patterns of the balustrade columns and that on the boards are different too.

Nobody will be blind to the richness that the curving river and the gracefulness of the bridges bring to the grave square. Nobody will be blind to the contrast and the harmony that the buildings and river present as a unity. Nobody will be blind to the creativeness the ancient architects demonstrated near 600 years ago.

No doubt the Inner Golden River has its functions. It had supplied constructions water, and water for daily cleaning in the old days. It also helped when people were putting off fires. It is still collecting rainwater through the drainage system today.

21. The Inner Forbidden Gates

The Forbidden City is divided into two areas at the square of *Qianqingmen* (Gate of Heavenly Purity) which is delimited at *Longzongmen* (Gate of Great Ancestors) in the west and *Jingyunmen* (Gate of Great Fortune) in the east.

Grand ceremonies were not quite often in the emperor's daily life, and the rear abode area was the place for him and his empress and concubines to spend most of their time. Apart from living, the emperor dealt with state affairs and met his ministers. Especially after the emperor of Qing dynasty move the space for court held at imperial gate from *Taihemen* to *Qianqingmen*, the inner court area became more important for royal life. On account of functional changes of the palace, offices for the Ministers, the Office of Princes and Dukes and the Grand Council of State were established, thus the inner abode area was actually changed into the inner court area. As the main entrances at both sides of the square, *Longzongmen* and *Jingyunmen* guarded the way to the inner area, so they were also called as the Inner Forbidden Gates. Even the nobles and the court officials were not allowed to trespass the gates unless summoned or on duty. In the year of 1782, Emperor Qianlong permitted military officials higher than Rank 2, civil officials no inferior than Rank 3 and those on duty to enter the city together with their entourages, but all the followers had to keep standing outside the Inner Forbidden Gates beyond 20 steps.

Strictly as the gates were guarded, they were not absolutely safe all the time. We still can see today an arrowhead left on the tablet of *Longzongmen*. The story took place in the 18th year of Emperor Jiaqing's reign (1813), when an insurrectionary army with help of eunuchs whose names were Liu Jin and Yan Jinxi fought into the Forbidden City and directly headed to *Yangxindian* (Hall of Mental Cultivation), and was hindered at the Gate. They shoot arrows at the guards of the Palace, but the guards had the firelocks and were much more in number, so that the rebellion was finally put to an end. During that time, Emperor Jiaqing was not in *Beijing*, and there was a great chaos in the capital until the emperor came back and published his Regretting Letter for his fault that caused the uprising. To remember this event, Jiaqing commanded to keep the arrowhead on the tablet as a lesson for more careful reign.

22. Story of Lion Couples in Front of the Palaces

Altogether 6 pairs of lions are placed on copper or stone pedestals in front of the important gates in the Forbidden City such as *Taihemen*, *Qianqingmen*, *Yangxinmen*, *Ningshoumen*, *Yangxingmen* and the courtyard of *Changchun* Palace. 5 of them are made of gilded-copper, and the other one is made of bronze at *Taihemen* (Gate of Great Har-

mony) which is the largest in size and the most delicate in decorations and holds the most significant position of them all. The pair of bronze lions has guarded the grand gate for centuries, shining simple but remote glories of history. The steady and modest bronze color suits the atmosphere of *Taihemen* well.

It is recorded that lion is not a local animal in China, but imported from Iran in Han dynasty (206 BC to 220 AD). As a beast of prey from abroad, the lion is extraordinarily esteemed and loved by vernacular people.

The spirit Lion got a special Chinese name *Suanni*, and legends tell that it can run 500 *li* (250 km) a day, its roar shakes the heaven and the earth, and it preys on tigers and wolves. It is no doubt the emperor of the kingdom of animals. It is naturally the symbol of power and strength, and has been taken advantage of to exorcize the evil. It is also an indispensable furnishing in front of palaces and courts, temples and government complexes. There also goes some old saying that from details of the lions, hierarchy system can also be seen to distinguish the status of the owner of the building. The most representative is the number of its hair buns. A lion of the highest grade has 13 buns, which was placed in front of the residence of the official of the first rank. Basing on this, officials of one rank lower would have a lion of one fewer buns on the head, and those below the 7th grade court rank were not allowed to have lions at the gate of residence.

Lion guards in the Forbidden City were made in Ming and Qing dynasties. They are decorative and expressive of dignity and supremacy of the emperor. Careful visitors will see that in each pair of the lions, the left one is different from the right. It is the male which is on the left of the gate facing outwardly, and the female on the right. Stretching out her left paw, the female is playing with her kid who is lying on the back happily deep in the joy of mother love, while the male puts his right paw on a ball made of strips. The female lion with her baby stands for flourishing offspring, and the male lion with the ball means handling the power of the empire.

23. The Plain but Significant Building for the Office of the Grand Council of State

Inside the inner Forbidden Gate *Longzongmen*, a row of plain buildings not eye-catching at all silently stand at the foot of the south wall of the inner abode area. Hardly can anyone guess out that it was one of the most significant places from where imperial edicts had been drafted and military commands had been sent and attracted the attention of all provinces. It was the office building for the Office of the Grand Council of State.

During emperor Yongzheng's reign, the border situation at the northwest was extremely tense, and the members of Grand Secretariat who took charge of military affairs were terribly occupied. But there was a defect that the Grand Secretariat was located in the complex of *Wenhuadian* (Hall of the Literary Glory), far from the inner court area. The diligent emperor found it quite inconvenient to keep himself informed in time of the current situation and make decision with the help of his cabinet. The reporting system was not effective either. Files were to pass several offices to reach those who were capable of dealing military affairs and the emperor, which was also likely to divulging top secrets. Thinking of all these factors, the emperor Yongzheng made up his mind to establish Junjichu, the Department of Confidential Military Affairs which later turned into the Grand Council of State.

In the first years of the department history, designated officials mainly concentrated on military affairs only, and the Grand Secretariat was the organization that dealt with routine national and palatial affairs. Gradually, as put on in many countries, the power and duty of Junjichu expanded so far as to interfere into imperial household affairs. On the other hand, grand secretaries farther from the power but yet of the high ranks had to while away the time by reading, painting and writing, so that Grand Secretariat was no more a power center but a academic organization, while the Junjichu actually became the Grand Council of State.

Officials of the Grand Council of State included 2 ranks, the Grand Minister of Council of State and Zhangjing (the secretary). Ministers were chosen by the emperor himself and the Zhangjing were selected from Palace examinations. There were 3 levels of ministers. The Top ministers were called Junji Dachen, or Grand Ministers, the second level were called Junji Dachen Xingzou, or the Probationary Grand Ministers, and the subordinate were Junji Dachen Xuexi Xingzou, or the Learning Probationary Ministers. There used to be one chief grand minister taking charge of the department, and Zhangjing's duty was secretary affairs.

Interior furnishings were rather simple inside the office of

Junjichu. Nothing but tables, chairs, beds and stationeries were placed. A tablet of emperor Yongzheng's calligraphy, *Yituanheqi* (literarily harmonious atmosphere), is now still hanging on the southern wall, and there is another tablet preserved on the east wall which was written by emperor Xianfeng. The characters are *Xibaohongjing* (good report announcing victory). In those years, in such simple office, Grand Ministers had to gather at 3 to 5 o'clock in the morning and would be summoned to see the emperor at 7 to 9. When reporting to the emperor face to face, the officials were usually seated, in fact half kneeling, on a so-called Junjidianzi, mattress especially used in Office of the Grand Council of State, to note the emperor's edicts that to be drafted, copied and re-inspected by the emperor and finally publicized. Zhangjing, the lower rank officials worked subordinately in the southern row of building inside *Longzongmen*.

There were many strict requirements to maintain secrecy in Junjichu. According to Qing regulations, subordinate officials had to collect and send documents personally, no willful entering was permitted, and grand ministers were forbidden to talk with people freely. When the emperor was talking with officials from Junjichu, no one else was allowed to be there. At any time documents were delivered form *Junjichu*, there were also some special requirements. Files, called *"Ting Ji"* (the court letter), should be sealed well and be sent through the court posts. The court letter that was traveled 300 to 500 *li* a day (150-250 km) was the ordinary kind, while the express mail would reach the provincial commander at the speed of 800 *li* a day, thus the linkage between central and local government was enhanced.

24. Palace Banquets

In Qing palace, banquets were held on the lunar New Year's Eve, the New Year's Day, the mid-Autumn Festival, the Winter Solstice Day, and birthday celebrations of the emperor and empress, etc. Among all these events, banquets for the New Year and the birthdays of the reining couple were the most ceremonious.

Before each event, it was required that the manager of the imperial kitchen should ask for the emperor's edict of time, place and participants of the banquet. In daily lives, the emperor had no body share his meals which he had twice everyday, breakfast in the morning and dinner in the afternoon, and maybe some leisure meals at his will. But in the banquets, he was to have a fix

entourage according to the rite, with his empress and concubines on the New Year's Eve, with his princes on the New Year's Day, and with Grand Ministers of Council of State and Grand Secretariats on the following day. The emperor would have 3 meals on the days of ceremony. It was carefully regulated what

was for the cold dish, hot dish, and dessert, what kind of tableware to use, and what to be displayed. The emperor's table was with no exception decorated with gold dragons and placed in the middle of the dinning hall. On the both sides, smaller tables for the entourages were numbered and categorized. Rites for the banquet were quite complicated and rather a burden than a real feast for the attendees. The tables on the left hand were superior to those on the right when looking from the point of the emperor. The empress and concubines or the nobles or the ministers had to follow the set order to take their seats first, waiting for the emperor's appearance. Any movement of the emperor and any dish serving were accompanied by music. No tiny violation would be forgiven. The hierarchy system was here once more clearly reflected.

As for the dishes, the sequence was usually from the cold to the hot, and then the milk tea. After changing the tableware, wines were served. Finally would be the fruits and another tea. All the serves and people's actions, taking food in and out the banquet began from the emperor and then from higher status to the inferior.

Dishes were cooked at the imperial kitchen, and tea kitchen by the most outstanding chefs from different nationalities, Manchu,Han and Hui. They all had their specialties. Their names were to be noted as each dish was served, so that the emperor would know who was his favorite and who would be given rewards.

25. The Emperor's Meals

Having meals is something common in our daily life, but in the imperial court, it is rather important and complicated. It requires a large department in the Inner Court to be in charge of such things according to the regulations of the Qing Dynasty. Meals are served strictly in correspondence with their ranks.

The Imperial Kitchen is the department for managing the food and meals of the imperial court that consisted of 80 members

or so subdivided into five levels. Another section under the Imperial Household Department was responsible for purchasing grains, meat, vegetables and other ingredients used for cooking.

An emperor usually had his meals at his private abode or somewhere he would regularly go. Anyhow, it was often changeable. General speaking, there were two meals a day. The breakfast was served from 6 to 7 o'clock and the dinner usually from 12 to 2 o'clock in the afternoon. Besides the two regular meals as above mentioned, snacks such as refreshments (pastries) and wine were offered at about 6 in the evening or at anytime when it was needed.

To the emperor, "food" was not called "food" but "viands", so "having a meal" was thus called "consuming the viands". When the meal was needed, the order of "transmitting the viands" would be soon passed down from the emperor's eunuch of the imperial presence to the eunuch on duty outside of the palace.

Immediately, the eunuchs for serving meals set the dinner table, carrying the dishes and food from the Imperial Kitchen and laid them on the table in order. Usually, the emperor had meals himself unless someone was especially invited to eat together with him. The empress and concubines always had their meals in their own palaces respectively. When the dishes were ready, a eunuch would be ordered to check whether the color of the small silver panels in the plates was changed or not for it was believed that poison can change the color of silver. Then, for the same reason, a eunuch must taste the dishes one by one to make sure that all food was safe and good. Finally, the emperor would start to have his meals.

The water used for imperial kitchen was the spring water taken from the Jade Spring Hill (Yuquanshan) and the rice was chosen from the areas of the Jade Spring Hill, Fengzeyuan and Tang Quan. Furthermore, tributes were also the main source of grain for the Imperial Palace. The mutton and milk were supplied by Qingfengsi (Department of the Imperial Pasturages) in the palace, while the chicken, ducks, fish, pork and fresh vegetables were bought from the market everyday. In addition, a variety of delicacies usually were the tributes from all parts of China.

The repast of the imperial family members in the Forbidden City including the emperor and empress were arranged according to the related regulations of the Qing Dynasty, The list of material used for the emperor's repast of a day is as follows: 11kg pork for cooking dishes, 2. 5kg meat for soup, 2 sheep, 5 chickens, 3 ducks, and 43kg variety of vegetables, 3kg Chinese onions, 125g wine, 1. 5kg thick sauce, 1. 5kg soy sauce. 1 kg sugar. In addition, there were 8 plates pastry served along with the dinner, each plate was 30 pieces. 50kg milk, 12 jars of spring water from the Jade Spring Hill, 500g cream, 75 packets of tea, each packet weighed 2 *liang*. All the materials valued 50 taels of silver.

From a record in the Qing archive, it is known that, on the 10th month of the 12th year of the emperor Qianlong's reign, the emperor had his supper in *Chonghuagong* (Palace of Double Glory), more than 20 courses and pastries were served on the dining table, including swallow nest and duck, chicken, pork, mutton, pheasant, roe deer, deer, etc. So much excessive food, of course, the emperor couldn't consume all by himself. The leftovers, in accordance with the Qing regulation, would be bestowed on concubines, princes and princesses and ministers. In the feudal society when the emperor's power was above everything else, the one who got such dishes from the emperor would feel a great honor.

26. Tea-Drinking in the Forbidden City

As one of the well-known special products of China, tea has a long history. By the Tang Dynasty, the first special book on tea titled *Chajing* (the Canon of Tea) written by Lu Yu was put out. In this book the writer made an introduction in detail about the subjects of tea including its characteristics, quality, producing area, picking and process, the infusing and boiling method, as well as the tea set.

The emperors of the Qing Dynasty were very interested in China's long history of tea culture, so drinking and sipping tea became the necessary in their daily life either at ordinary time or at grand banquets.

Most of the tea drunk by the Qing emperor and empress

came mainly from the tributes that was produced in different areas of the whole country.

As can be read in archives of the Qing court, there were many kinds of teas well-contained in a variety of canisters, such as *Longjing* (Dragon Well) tea, *Yuqian* tea (picked before Grain Rain—the 6th of the 24 solar terms), *Mengshanding* (picked on the top of the Meng Mountain) tea, *Zhulan* tea, *Songluo* tea, *Chun* (Spring) tea, *Anhua Ya* tea, *Ganyichu* tea, and so on.

The tea sets for the daily use of the emperor and empress usually made of jade, silver, porcelain and *Zisha* were precious and tasteful, either in excellent workmanship or in refined and elegant shapes. Sometimes you can even find the verses composed by emperors on some of these articles.

It is different from our way of infusing tea with hot water, that the people in the Qing court would prefer boiling tea with fire in earthenware pot or copper pot. The boiled tea, with strong red color and mellow taste, would be poured into the teapot for drinking at anytime.

The water used for boiling tea in the court was gotten from Jade Spring Hill (Yuquanshan) 30 *li* away from the Beijing City. Because of that the spring water was sweet and refreshing, it was conferred the title of "the First Spring Water under the Heaven" by the Emperor Qianlong. The tea boiled with such water could send forth a best sweet-smelling taste.

Tea as a kind of healthy drink has indeed the effect for promoting the secretion of saliva and helping digestion. Drinking tea as a tasteful cultural activity not only may provide you a wonderful treat but also bring you a good health.

27. **Wine-Drinking in the Qing Court**

In the Qing Dynasty, wine for the use of emperor in the court was mainly the Yuquan (Jade Spring) wine. In addition, there were also some other wines for daily use, such as the Tusu wine, Xionghuang wine, Yellow wine and so on.

Yuquan wine was so named because the water used for making it derived from Yuquanshan (Jade Spring Hill). Emperor Qianlong once regarded this water as the first spring under the heaven for its sweet and refreshing taste. Besides being used to make wine, the spring water was also the drinking water for the emperor's daily use whether he was in the Court, going out for an inspecting tour, or hunting.

The formula for making Yuquan (jade spring) wine, a spirit of less alcohol content, is as fellows: 90 *jin* (a unit of traditional Chinese weight) of wine was made of glutinous rice 1 *dan* (a unit of dry measure for grain), huai-leaven 7 *jin* (a unit of traditional Chinese weight), bean-leaven 8 *jin*, Chinese prickly ash 8 *qian* (a unit of traditional Chinese weight), yeast 8 *liang* (a unit of traditional Chinese weight), bamboo leaf 4 *liang* and sesame seed 4 *liang*.

After the period of Emperor Qianlong's reign, *Yuquan* wine gradually became the main wine for the use of the emperor either at ordinary times or on festivals. The amount of wine drunk by emperors vary in quantity from 7 to 15 *liang* a day. According to the related documents, the Qing Emperor Jiaqing drank the Taiping wine 4 *liang*, and Yuquan wine 10 *liang* on the 16th, a warmly fine day, of the fifth lunar month in 1804 (the 9th year of the emperor Jiaqing's reign).

On important occasions and festivals in the court, a lot of wine was to be expended. For instance, on his birthday the 6th day of the 10th lunar month every year, the emperor Jiaqing would drink Yuquan wine about 3 or 4 *jin*. In 1785 (the 50th year of the Qianlong's reign) and 1796 (the first year of Jiaqing's reign), the emperor Qianlong held grand Qiansouyan (Banquet for thousand aged men) respectively in *Qianqinggong* (Palace of Heavenly Purity) and *Huangjidian* (Hall of Imperial Supremacy), each of which expended Yuquan wine 400 *jin* for 800 banquet tables on the average.

Besides being a kind of drink, the Yuquan wine was also the preference in imperial kitchens as the cooking wine. For example, the kitchen serving the Empress Dowager Cixi, would consume 37. 5 *jin* per month.

On the occasions of important memorial ceremonies, such as the late emperors' birthday, the anniversary of late emperors' death, the Dragon Boat Festival (the 5th day of the 5th lunar month), the Double Ninth Festival (the 9th day of the 9th lunar month) and Qing Ming Festival (the 5th of the 24 solar terms), the Yuquan wine, as the symbol of good future, was usually offered in *Fengxiandian* (Hall of Worshipping Ancestors) according to the sacrificial rites. Sometimes, this wine was also bestowed to officials or eunuchs by the emperor for expressing his favor.

Meanwhile, there were some other kinds of wines used for different purposes in the court, such as Tusu wine for driving off the plaque; Xionghuang wine for detoxicating the snake-poison; Wujiapi wine having the efficacy to rheumatism. Some times, several wines were mixed together for drinking.

  1*dan*＝1hectolitre
  1*jin*＝16*liang*＝500g
  1*liang*＝16*qian*

28. History of Smoking in the Imperial Court

Tobacco planting arose originally in Spain in 1559, and soon became fashionable throughout the Europe. During the early days of the 17th century, tobacco was introduced into China. At first it was planted in Zhangzhou areas of Fujian Province and rapidly spread all over the both sides of the Yangtze River. Up to the late Ming and early Qing Period, smoking pipes was already very popular in the country.

About the same time when tobacco was introduced into China, the snuff was also introduced along with it. According to related report, the Italy missionary Matteo Ricci once paid the snuff as the tribute to the Emperor Wanli of the Ming Dynasty. Manufacturing snuff was a very complicated process and quite high priced. In addition, it needed to use a fine snuff-bottle, so, in a long period, only imperial family members could enjoy it. Up to the Qing Dynasty, snuffing tobacco began to spread among the people because the Manchurians had usually had this habit before seizing the state power from the hands of Hans of the Ming Dynasty.

Since the Kangxi's reign, snuffing tobacco in the Qing Court was accepted gradually and being current in the Qianlong and Jiaqing period. On the other hand, snuff was often used as the bestowal by the emperor. Snuffing among the emperor, empress and concubines continued into the Daoguang's reign. Furthermore, the popularity of snuffing not only promoted the production of the snuff but also stimulated the production of snuff bottles. A great variety of the snuff bottles with exquisite workmanship have exerted a strong fascination upon the Western connoisseurs of art.

By the late Qing Dynasty, it may relate to the individual hobby of the Empress Dowager Cixi, to smoke water pipe subsequent to the tobacco and snuff rising in the imperial court.

In the last years of the Qing Dynasty, the western cigarette flowed into the Chinese market. Compared with tobacco, snuff or water pipe, the cigarette is more simple and convenient. In addition, cigarette smoking was regarded to be more gentlemanly and to have a higher civilization. So, the cigarette soon replaced the snuff and water pipe in the court. Puyi, the abdicated emperor once bought a large number of western best brands of cigarettes for the reason of that cigarette-smoking had become one of his hobbies.

29. Having *Jiaozi* (dumplings) in Imperial Palace

Jiaozi, or dumplings with meat and vegetable stuffing, is a favorite food for the northerners of China. The method to prepare *Jiaozi* is: making the dough into small round *Jiaozi* wrappers, putting stuffing in it, folding it in two, and pinching its rim together tightly. According to the different cookery, it's respectively called "boiled *Jiaozi*", "steamed *Jiaozi*" and "lightly fried *Jiaozi*". Meanwhile, *Jiaozi* is also called "flat food", "water pastry" and *"Bobo"*.

Jiaozi in China has a long history. As early as the Jin Dynasty, *Jiaozi* was popular among the people. But it was named *Huntun* (dumpling soup) then. Up to the Qing period, *Jiaozi* has already become a kind of more popular food and a symbol of

the auspices and happiness. So, eating *Jiaozi* is indispensable on many occasions, such as the day before an oldman's birthday, the wedding ceremony of the young, and the New Year's Day.

As same as the custom to eat *Jiaozi* among the common people, the Qing emperors were very glad to enjoy it as well. Even in the regulations of the wedding ceremony of the Qing emperors, there was especially the article about eating *Jiaozi*. On Spring Festivals, having *jiaozi* in the Qing court not only meant a welcome to the new year's coming, but even more important, expressed their sincere heart never to forgot their ancestors, on account of that the Manchu people had had the habit of eating frozen *jiaozi* before they occupied the Beijing city. At 12 (midnight) on the New Year's Eve, a point of solemn time, the emperor had to perform a series of sacrificing ceremonies before having *jiaozi*. In addition, on the New Year's Day, the vegetarian *jiaozi*, for worshipping Buddhas, had to be boiled together with those for emperor at the same time and in same pot. After the emperor had his meal (*jiaozi*), eunuchs then put other *jiaozi* in dishes and offered them on the table in front of Buddha shrines. In the "Archives on Foods" of the Qing court. We can read: "on the New Year's Day of the lunar calendar, in *Yangxindian* (Hall of Metal Cultivation) the emperor Guangxu had his meal totaled 26 *jiaozi*, half of them were stuffed with pork and vegetable and the others were stuffed with pork and spinach".

30. The Icebox Used in the Imperial Palace

Today, the refrigerator has become a kind of necessary appliance in our daily life. However, long before the refrigerator appeared, how did the people keep the foods fresh in the imperial court of the Qing Dynasty during sweltering days? As it turns out, the "icebox" was also used in the palace. It's of course not the refrigerator like ours today, but in fact relies on the natural ice to lower the temperature inside of the box.

In the collections of the Palace Museum, there are several iceboxes once used in the Qing court, among which is an icebox of cloisonne enamel that looks very beautiful and exquisite. It is

about half meter high. The top and the bottom are all in the square shapes; the length of sides is 66 cm or 82 cm respectively. The outer layer of it is made of cloisonne enamel decorated with rosette design. Its wooden body is covered with a layer of lead for the purpose of keeping temperature and protecting from the moisture. A small round hole at the bottom of the icebox is used for draining off the water when the ice inside has melted. In the meantime, the cold air can flow out of two ancient-coin-shaped holes on the cover of it. In fact, such an icebox has not only the practical value but also is an elegant and gorgeous furnishing in the palace.

Most of the iceboxes used in the Qing court were made of wood and also called ice tubs. On the one hand, it can be used for keeping food fresh in the hot summer days, and on the other hand it can lower the temperature in the room by the aid of cold air flowing out of the holes on the surface of the icebox. Although such kinds of iceboxes look to be very primitive, they actually have the double function of a refrigerator and an air condition.

31. Ancient Chronometer
in Imperial Palace

Chronometer was a crucial device for daily life and various purposes in the imperial palace. What had been used to regulate the emperor's, the son of the Heaven's life, meals, ceremonies and holding court?

It can be read in historical archives and remaining relics that the device varies from traditional Chinese sundial and copper clepsydra to western clocks made in England or France and some in China by domestic craftsmen.

The sundial is archaic and turned into a furnishing taking on stronger ceremonious color. There are 2 kinds of sundials, the equatorial plane sundial and the horizontal sundial. The former was most frequently used inside the Forbidden City among which the one in front of *Taihedian* (Hall of Great Harmony) is a typical example. It has a stone pedestal, a round stone dial plate placed at an angle of inclination, and a copper pointer in the middle perpendicular to the plate. From the direction and length of the shadow of the pointer, ancient people could tell the time.

Copper clepsydra is quite archaic too. It was invented in China 3,000 years ago. Sending forth vernacular flavor, clepsydra is built in a pavilion. It has 5 clepsydrae installed from the top to the bottom. There are 3 water containers arranged in a row on the top, which are all called suppliers, below the second supplier is a distributor, and at the bottom is the water collector. When it works, the first supplier at the highest position is full of water, and giving water out from a dragon mouth in the front of the container to the second supplier, then the third, and then to the distributor. The distributor separates water and let drops go into the collector. Inside the collector is a copper figure holding an arrow pointer that indicates the time. The arrow is carried up and down with a so-called arrow boat floating on the surface of the water in the collector.

Another traditional chronometer in the Forbidden City is chime clock, which strikes at every hour sharp. Some of the chime clocks made in the mid period of Qing dynasty are still preserved in the Palace Museum. These clocks are evidence of cultural and scientific exchange between China and the West in history. Exterior of the clocks are Chinese pavilions, while the interior structure, mechanic principles, and hours setting were all from western countries. Surprisingly enough, those clocks older than 200 years still work and strike precisely today.

Qing court had extensive uses of various clocks, domestic and foreign. Some were presents or imported from England, France and Switzerland. The foreign clocks are of astonishingly variety of shapes, styles and way of working. They were for placing on the desk, hanging on the wall, in the bed-curtain, or putting in the pockets or at the waistband. They were practical and decorative, and in some cases, even amusing.

32. For What the Bell and Drum Toll

Traditionally a night is divided into 5 *Jing*, that is 5 2-hour periods according to modern watch. The 1st *Jing* announces the dusk, and the 5thwelcomes the dawn, as the old saying goes, *the 3rdJing, the dead of night*. In the old city of Beijing, the night watchman beats the clapper or gong during the night, and towers were also built for beating drums to tell the time. The Forbidden City was not exceptional. It was used to give all the residents, the emperor, empress, concubines and all the servants the correct time.

Shenwumen, the north gate of the Forbidden City was actually a drum tower for giving the time. There was a drum inside the building of the gate on the base, and a guard on duty every night. Apart from the drum, a large bell was also hung there. Every night when the emperor was not living in the city, bell was to be beaten 108 times before the drum announced the 1st *Jing*. And at dawn the next, after the 5th*Jing* another 108 times bell beat was repeated. 108 is the number gotten by adding the 12 months, 24 Chinese solar divisions and 72 *hou* divisions together. According to *the Canon of Rites of Qing Dynasty*, guards should be on duty in turn at every Tower of Drum and Bell, beat at every *Jing* sharp, but the eunuchs should look after the bell and drum on *Shenwumen* (Gate of Martial Spirit), and be on duty every night. In the 61ˢᵗ year of emperor Kangxi's reign (1722), imperial edict claimed that honor guards take over the task of beating the drum in the night at *Shenwumen*.

No matter how strictly the rule was carried out, mistake was inevitable. The recorded accident was a day in the late 7ᵗʰ month according to Chinese lunar calendar in 1726, when emperor Yongzheng was reading over official papers by the light in the mid night and a wrong beat of drum came into the ears of the emperor. Right the next morning, edict was made to find out the derelict and put him to punishment.

Besides *Shenwumen*, *Wumen* (Meridian Gate) also has a bell pavilion and a drum pavilion on the both wings, but the devices here were not for claiming the time, but for ceremonious purposes. As the front entrance of the Forbidden City, there were ritual rules for beating bell and drum to accompany the emperor's appearance. The bell tolled when the emperor went out to sacrifice at the Altar for the God of Land and Grain, and the drum was beaten when he worshipped at the ancestral temple. During the grand ceremonies at *Taihedian* (Hall of Great Harmony), such as mounting the throne, New Year's Celebration, Winter Solstice Day, the emperor's birthday and titling the empress, the bell and drum on *Wumen* were to be beaten simultaneously.

33. Lighting in the Forbidden City

For the Emperor and Empress who lived in the Forbidden City, the lighting at night was much more important than that for the ordinary people who lived in the primitive society. In fact, lamp and lanterns were not only the necessary for their luxurious daily life in the imperial court, but also the symbol of the highest social status of the imperial family.

The lights used in the Forbidden City were mainly the palace lanterns in different shapes of square, round, hexagon, fan-shape, some of which were decorated with a canopy on the shade, and others with silk tassels or auspicious pendants. The materials for making lanterns were gilt-copper, cloisonne enamel, carved-lacquer, hardwood or rhi-noceros-horn. Some lanterns were inlaid with glasses or covered with stretched gauze, on which paintings or verses would be easily found.

In the lanterns, candles were always fixed. When the land was enveloped in a curtain of darkness, the lanterns would be lighted and hung in the room or set on the table for responding to the different needs. On the other hand, they were also a part of decorations in the palaces. On the occasion from the 24th day of the last month every lunar year to the 15th of the first month of the next year, lanterns hung in the Forbidden City would be much more colorful and exquisite so as to celebrate the traditional Lantern Festival.

In addition, the copper road lamps were installed in front of gates of halls and palaces. Such lamps were set on a marble base and covered with a copper pavilion-shaped shade inlaid with glass sheets around all sides, protecting from either the wind or the rain. All the ordinary persons in the Forbidden City lighted their way with the help of such road lamps at nights except the princes, noble dukes and ministers, who could be allowed to carry the ox-horn lanterns to lead their way.

The lighting regulations in the palace were extremely strict during the Ming and Qing Dynasties. For example, the road lamps mentioned above were only permitted to be installed inside the imperial palace; any other place or people were forbidden to use them.

In the late Qing Dynasty, electricity replaced the candle as the major source of lighting in the Forbidden City. The Empress Dowager Cixi installed generators in the City to meet the lighting requirements of the inner court. As well as the electric lamps instead of the candles, a lot of new type of lamps would appear. By the period of abdicated emperor Puyi, not only a variety of wall and desk lamps but some large hanging lights were also installed in the Forbidden City.

34. Imperial Bridal Chamber

In Ming dynasty, *Kunninggong* (Palace of Earthly Tranquility) was the main abode palace for the empress. Later in Qing dynasty, it was changed into a space for religious purpose and only leaving the east room for the imperial bridal chamber. After the honeymoon, the empress might choose any of the 12 palace complexes in the east and west of the rear area as her residence. Status quo of *Kunninggong* now shows the original scene of emperor Guangxu's nuptial room.

Warm and happy we can describe ordinary people's bridal chambers, and what can we say about the imperial one?

As a routine, according to the rites, the imperial couple would enter the nuptial chamber after drinking the wedding cup and having the buns for prosperous offspring on the wedding banquet. Right inside the door leafs with gold décor and characters of "Shuangxi" (double happiness) a big lantern with double happiness decors was hung. At both the west and east doors to the chamber was a red screen with golden double happiness pattern, which auspiciously means run in to good fortune and happiness when opening the door. The chamber itself inside the east cozy room is not larger than 10 square meters. By the north wall an imperial seat is placed with a *Ruyi*, a propitious artifact, on the right hand, and with emperor Xianfeng's calligraphy works at the back on the wall. Along the south, there is a *kang*, a long and wide bed built with bricks and timber structure, and on each end along the *kang*, are red sandalwood carvings with dragon and phoenix designs. Small wares as porcelain and enamel vases are all placed on the tables, and paintings and calligraphies on the walls. The nuptial bed is at the north wall. Red cotton-padded mattress, satin quilts and pillows are all of dragon and phoenix patterns and double happiness, moreover the satin bed curtain is embroidered with 100 little boys, hoping that the emperor would have prosperous offspring. Inside the bed on the wall are a pair of couplets, a painting of peony and a delicate shelf for little objects. Treasures are hidden in the drawers, red lights are reflected at each corner, and happiness permeates everything. The last emperor Puyi wrote in his book *My Early Years*, *Red curtains, red mattress, red clothes, red skirts, red flowers and red cheeks, everything and everything were just like a puddle of melt red wax.* From these words, we can comprehend his comprehensive feelings, so that we may imagine the warm atmosphere in the bridal chamber.

35. Inner Palaces for Imperial Concubines

No one can tell what was the first time the saying prevailed that the emperor has 3 palaces, 6 courtyards for his 72 concubines. Is it true? Where are the palaces and courtyards?

The Forbidden City had been the imperial palace during Ming and Qing dynasties. Its layout strictly follows the traditional rule of Front Court and Rear Abode. The front court is the office buildings for ceremonies and reining affairs, while the rear part is the so called 3 palaces and 6 courtyards. It is the Ming arrangement that used the 3 palaces in the rear area along

the middle axis for abode, and allotted the 6 east palaces and 6 west palaces at both sides to the imperial concubines. Obviously enough, the even number 6 was selected for the feminine while odd numbers as 9 was for the masculine. But is the saying of 72 imperial concubines true?

Emperors in history had various numbers of concubines. We may raise the emperors of Qing dynasty for example. There were altogether 8 grades of imperial concubines according to the regulations, including the empress who takes charge of all inner feminine affairs, one Huangguifei, 2 Guifei, 4 Fei, 6 Pin, and much inferior, Guiren, Changzai and Daying without regular numbers. Though the high rank imperial concubines summed up to 14, but it is not fixed. As for emperor Kangxi, he had 33 ladies of high ranks, and much more of lower status. The only common custom was that the emperor should have one empress at a time. Early emperor of Qing dynasty had more concubines than the later ones. In the 16th year of emperor Kangxi's reign, 1 empress, 1 Guifei and 7 Pin were titled, but in the late period, emperor Guangxu only had 1 empress and 2 Fei.

Empress entitlement has 3 different ways. The first was when the emperor got old enough to get married, the spouse would be carefully selected, and after the grand wedding ceremony, she was to be formally titled the empress. The second

way was through promotion. Huang-guifei, Guifei, Fei and Pin all had chance to be promoted to the status of empress. The other way was entitlement posthumous. It is not a surprise that the successive emperor was not born by the empress, thus in many cases after he mounted the throne, he was sure to confer his late mother the empress.

Other high rank imperial concubines' entitlements were quite similar to that of the empress, except that there was no ceremony held. Each lady higher than Pin would receive a gold album and a gold seal, and Pin would not have the seal. It is also imaginable that the fates of imperial concubines were in the hand of the emperor, some might be promoted, some degraded and some were even consigned to limbo. Enjoying glory and luxury though, imperial concubines would have to endure long loneliness unless they could possibly win the emperor's favor. Some were selected into the palace at blossoming age, but withered at the same time at the sudden death of the emperor, and never escaped the palace as widows.

36. Sacrificing Ceremonies inside the Forbidden City

Inside the Forbidden City, there had been specific spaces for worshipping the God and ancestors, respectively *Kunninggong* (Palace of Earthly Tranquility) and *Fengxiandian* (Hall of Worshipping Ancestors).

Kungninggong had been the main abode palace for the empress in Ming dynasty. Later the Qing emperors titled it the same way, but actually no empress had ever lived there. The reason was when *Kunninggong* was rebuilt in early Qing dynasty, the interior layout and exterior style was readjusted according to the customs of Manchu, which is obviously different from other palaces that were built after the style of the Han. The most distinguishable characteristic is that the door is not open in the central bay of the building but at the east so as to form a large interior space in the west. Inside this room, the *kang* was built along the south, west and north walls enveloping the sacrificing space for the God of Manchu.

Sacrificing activities were quite often in *Kunninggong*. There were morning and evening sacrificing everyday besides grand movements. Daily offerings were carried out by a prayer, an incense man and an offering chef. When grand sacrificing came, the emperor and the empress would attend personally. The spirits worshipped include Sakyamuni, General Guan Yu, Mongolia God, etc, while the offerings include cake, wine, pork and songs accompanied with plucked instruments of *Sanxian* (three string) and, *pipa*, drum and clapper. 4 pigs were used for daily offering and 39 for the grand ceremony in spring and autumn. Every year 700 *dan* (1 *dan* = 1 hectolitre) glutinous millets were consumed to brew alcohol, regardless of the cakes. Offerings and the ceremony of participants' sharing the offerings took place in the large interior space inside *Kunninggong*. We still can see in the hall the butcher's knife, chopping block and the cauldron used at that time.

It is a tradition that all the emperors sincerely esteem their ancestors. Apart from the ancestral temple built to the southeast of the Forbidden City, they had an inner ancestral temple to the east of the main rear palaces in the city. It was used for frequent consecration to the shrines. On the first and the 15th day of every lunar month and especially before the New Year's Day, the Winter Solstice Day, the emperor's birthday and other grand ceremonies, emperors of Qing dynasty would attend the sacrificing ceremony himself. What's more, on the anniversary of death birth and other holidays as Pure Brightness Day and Mid-Autumn, he would also be there to salute and express his grief and memories. Every time the emperor went hunting and every time fresh fruit and vegetables were on time, offerings to the imperial ancestors were obligatory, which is called "Jianxin" in mandarin, means offering the Fresh.

37. The Emperor on the New Year's Day

The Spring Festival, also called the lunar New Year's Day, is the most important traditional festival in China. During the joyous days, the people of the whole nation would hold the varied and colorful celebration activities, so as to express their feelings of joy and their best wishes on the New Year. In the imperial palace, the lunar New Year's Day, as one of the three major festivals, was also grandly celebrated.

The Qing emperor, on that very day, would give a series of sacrificial ritual activities to the gods and ancestors. The whole day's schedule for him was very heavy and full. It is as follows: at first, in a quite early time on that day before dawn, just at zero o'clock in the middle night, the emperor would get up, an hour later he would go by a sedan chair to the Imperial Garden to offer incense for the God of Zhen Wu in *Qin'andian* (Hall of Imperial Peace) and Dou Mu in *Chengruiting* (Pavilion of Clear and Auspiciousness); then came back to *Qianqinggong* (Palace of Heavenly Purity) to have a rest. About at two o'clock in the night, he would ride in a large sedan chair again to *Fengxiandian* (Hall of Worshipping Ancestors) for offering sacrifices to ancestors, then, let his mind relax in *Yangxindian* (Hall of Mental Cultivation). About three forty in the morning, he would go to *Kunninggong* (Palace of Earthly Tranquility) by an open sedan chair to perform Kowtow rites. After that he needed to go to the eastern side-room of The Palace of Heavenly Purity to offer incense; also, the same Kowtow rites would be acted in front of the sage (Confucian) portraits in the eastern link-room of the Palace of Heavenly Purity and the King of Medicine in the Imperial Medicine House respectively. Then the emperor returned to the Palace of Heavenly Purity to have milk tea, and then to the *Hongde* Hall to eat *Jiaozi* (dumplings). Successively, the emperor would go to offer sacrifices to the Buddhas in *Tangzi*, *Zhongzheng* Hall, *Jianfugong* (Palace for the Establishment of Happiness) and *Chonghuagong* (Palace of Double Glory). At six o'clock in the morning, the emperor with princes and high-ranking officials would go to *Ci'ninggong* (Palace of Compassion and Tranquility) to act the congratulation rite to the Empress Dowager. At seven, before the grand ceremony of celebrating New Year's Day was to be held in *Taihedian* (Hall of Great Harmony), the emperor always went to

Zhonghedian (Hall of Middle Harmony) to receive the greetings from his Grand Secretariat officials and then he would ascend on the throne in Hall of Great Harmony to have the New Year's greeting from the princes, dukes and ministers, as well as the civil and military officials. When the grand ceremony was over, the emperor still came back to the Palace of Heavenly Purity.

In *Qianqinggong* (Palace of the Heavenly Purity), the high ranking imperial concubines headed by the empress would pay a New Year's congratulation rite to the emperor, then, the emperor went to the Palace of Double Glorious to receive the same rite from his lower ranking consorts. When these necessary formalities had been done, the emperor would change into another suit of robe and eat breakfast with the empress and imperial concubines together.

After breakfast, the emperor would go out of *Shenwumen* (Martial Gate) to the Hall of *Dagao* in *Jingshan* Hill to do Kowtow rite, then rode the sleigh to the Temples of *Hongren* and the Temple of *Chanfu* on the west bank of the *Beihai* lake for worshiping Buddhas respectively, and next, came back to the *Shouhuang* Hall in the *Jingshan* Hill for offering sacrifices to the ancestors. After finishing the various prayers, the emperor returned to the Forbidden City.

At high noon, the 12 o'clock, the emperor would attend the grand New Year's banquet spread in *Qianqinggong* (Palace of Heavenly Purity). On either side of the emperor's table were some other tables at which princes sat according to their ranks. When the emperor took his place the court music *Zhong He Shao Yue* would be played. When the grand banquet started, cold dishes were served first, main dishes next, and then the tables would be replaced with the feast of wines and foods. At this time princes would hold a cup of wine in their hands kneeling before the emperor to give a toast to him. Then the Emperor invited companies to drink. After the feast of wines, the tea and fruit would be served on the table. Affer this, the grand banquet was finally finished, and the Emperor left The Palace of Heavenly Purity to return to the Hall of Mental Cultivation.

In the afternoon, the Emperor would have some drinking and foods at about 5 o'clock, on this occasion, the whole New Year's celebrating activities would be regarded as lowering its curtain.

38. The Figure "9" with Ancient Buildings and in the Ritual Customs

Wandering among the splendid ancient palaces, the odd number, especially the figure "9" used in the décor of the buildings and furnishings must impress ones deep sense. In the Ming Dynasty, the Beijing City had 9 city gates; the Tower of the *Tian'anmen* has 9 bays in breadth; in the Imperial Palace, on each halve of the gate, large or small, all bear 81 gilt bronze bosses in 9 rows, and each row has 9 bosses; the Chinese legend goes that the dragon has 9 sons; inside of the *Xiqing* Gate, the famous Nine Dragon Screen stands there; even steps leading to a hall or a terrace is also consisted of 9 or the multiple numbers of 9 steps.

So much "9" appeared in the Forbidden City, it is absolutely not an accidental coincidence. As one of the folkways of our nation, the number "9" is regarded as the largest masculine figure. So, "9" in the ancient culture of China, usually embodies the idea of "the most", "the largest" and "the utmost". For examples, the vast territory of our country was described "the 9 divisions" in ancient time. The highest heaven was described "the 9 levels heaven"; the deepest earth was "nine springs" (the nether world); the patriarchal clan system was called the degrees of 9 kindred", etc. All the cases as mentioned above proves that "9" is the symbol of the most lofty, the paramount honor and the greatest extent.

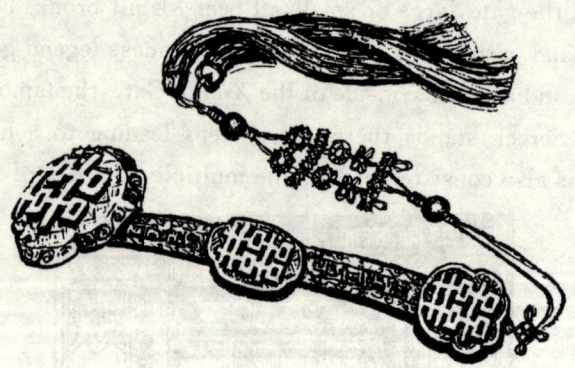

In addition, in a variety of rituals of celebrating activities held in the imperial palace, "9" was also necessary. Such as in the ceremony, one ought to perform the courtesy of kneeling three times and kowtowing 9 times. If tributes were presented to the emperor they must be 9 or a multiple of 9 pieces; in grand banquets, courses served must consist of 99 dishes; for celebrating the emperor's birthday the programs must have 99 items. For instance, on the occasion of the Emperor Qianlong's mother, the Empress Dowager Xiaosheng's 60 birthday, the gifts presented for the grand celebration at the first day were 9 Buddha statues, 9 pairs of palace lanterns, 9 agate vases, 9 jade objects, 9 pieces of ancient copper wares, 9 boxes of assorted fruits and candies, 9 hanging scrolls, 9 albums and 9 handscrolls. On the second day, the gifts would be 9 glass wares, 9 large ivory potted landscapes, 9 pairs of small table for burning incense, 9 *Ruyi* scepters of jade and agate, 9 plates of beeswax fruits, 9 boxes of perfume, 9 hand warmer of colored lacquer, 9 calabash carvings and 9 ivory decorations. Obviously, "9" in ancient Chinese conventions is representative of the supreme and utmost glory. Meanwhile, it also symbolizes longevity. So, the figure "9" became the exclusive possession of the emperor. No one, even high ranking official or noblelord, was allowed to use this number in his daily life or ritual activities. Whoever dares to run counter to the regulation must be punished for his disrespect.

39. *Yangxindian* and
its Important Position

After visiting the front and the 3 rear palaces, almost all the visitors are likely to see *Yangxindian* (Hall of Mental Cultivation). The hall is important in Qing history. It is the place where 8 emperors lived and dealt with state affairs and where many most significant events were brewed or took place. Not at all surprising, it is also a place extremely familiar to both scholars and amateurs on China's history.

It was a tradition of Ming dynasty that the emperor should live in *Qianqinggong* (Palace of Heavenly Purity), until emperor Yongzheng moved out in early Qing dynasty. The story began when Yongzheng's father emperor Kangxi died. Yongzheng had to follow the traditional rule to remain mourning at *Yangxin-*

dian, so he did not move in to *Qianqinggong* where the former emperor had lived for 60 years. But coincidently as well as certainly, he set up the example of living and working in *Yangxindian* other than *Qianqinggong* ever since.

We still can imagine today many reason for Yongzheng's decision. The first might be its convenient location for living. *Yangxindian* is situated at the south end of the first inner lane in the west of rear area, adjacent to the imperial kitchen to the south, and facing the west gate to *Qianqinggong*. It can be described as a linking point between the abode area and the ceremony area and has the functional advantage for meal service. On the other hand, the border situation was not peaceful during emperor Yongzheng's reign, especially at the northwest, so he decided to set up *Junjichu*, the Department of Confidential Military Affairs (later The Grand Council of state) whose office was located right outside the south gate of the west first inner lane. In the days of snow-like urgent military reports, where else could be a better place for the emperor than *Yangxindian* that is within minutes of walk from the military office? The convenience of meeting his military ministers might be one of the most important considerations of emperor Yongzheng.

The status of *Yangxindian* was promoted among the most grandeur halls for emperor Yongzheng's abode. Not only the decoration became the most delicate, but also the interior arrangement inside was designed according to functional requirements. The front hall of *Yangxindian* had been used as the office of comprehensive purposes, and the back building as the living rooms and bedrooms. In the middle room of the front hall, a throne is placed above which hangs a caisson ceiling. It was the space for the emperor to meet his ministers. There is a passage behind the screen of the throne, linking the hall with the living room. The east room of the front hall remains the scene when the Empress Dowager Cixi reined country behind curtain, handling the emperor Tongzhi and Guangxu. The west room had been the space for the emperor commenting on official papers and calling in his confidential ministers. Furniture and stationeries are all displayed according to the historical records. The wooden screen set outside the room was for safety purpose, so that the room was hidden from all possible peeps. In the west of the front hall, a small study room of 4 square meters called *Sanxitang* (Study of Three Rarities) is most famous nationwide. It is most famous for the collection of three rare pieces of calligraphic works.

Though *Yangxindian* is not large in scale, it is well designed and met all functional needs at the right place in the right time. This is why emperor Yongzheng chose it for living, why it holds a significant place in the history of Chinese architecture, and why it is a place visitor can never miss it.

40. Reining Behind the Curtain

It is a well-known historic event that the Empress Dowager Cixi reined the empire behind a curtain in late Qing dynasty. Inside the east room of the front hall of *Yangxindian* (Hall of Mental Cultivation), every interior detail is displayed to show the original scene of that story. The roles were Empress Dowager Cixi and Ci'an. But why and how did the story come into being?

The leading role was Empress Dowager Cixi who worked as the direct as well. At the death of emperor Xianfeng, Cixi did not recess into the palace for the empress dowagers, but by controlling her son in childhood, who was now the new emperor, she was able to wipe out the grand ministers selected by the late emperor who were still in her way. She prepared the enthroning ceremony for her son as she propagandized the legality of empress dowager's assisting reining behind curtain. When the plan came true, Cixi made herself the only real empress Dowager in Qing dynasty. Another factor leading Cixi to the protagonist was empress dowager Ci'an who was taciturn and not well literate. Superficially, the 2 empress dowagers were together assisting the young emperor, but in fact, Ci'an had to rely on Cixi reading out all the memorials to her, thus the power of monarchy fell into the sole hand of Cixi. Emperor Tongzhi died in his 20s, and emperor Guangxu succeeded. Cixi went to the back of the curtain again with the same strategy. Altogether she handled the country for 48 years.

In historical archives, no detail of the scene at both sides of the curtain was recorded except rendering in unofficial stories and novels.

We had better deduce from reliable materials than dream in the conflicting tales if our goal is reaching the truth. According to the *Actual Records of Mu'zong* (Emperor Tongzhi) and diaries of the ministers called upon by Cixi, the 2 empress dowagers and the emperor went to *Yangxindian* together. The old ladies sat behind a yellow curtain hung at the back of the seating of the child emperor, facing to the west. Like a puppet sat Emperor Tongzhi in front of the curtain. Then came the ministers and salutes as usual. After the regencies' permission, the minister would kneel down on mattresses to answer the questions. They could not see the empress dowagers' faces, except that their voices could be heard.

The curtain, as a prop, blocked the male and female,

separated the interior from the exterior. It was China's tradition that imperial concubines could not see the outsiders, and could not be seen as well, even in grand congratulating ceremonies. On the empress's birthday, ministers came and celebrated without seeing the empress either. It was quite natural for the empress regency to rein the country but behind a curtain. It was a fashion, a tradition, and above all, an all-accepted regulation for Chinese people at that time.

41. Auxiliary Building of *Yangxindian*

Apart from *Yangxindian* (Hall of Mental Cultivation), there are many auxiliary buildings inside the courtyard. All the buildings had functions and styles to follow, and because of the rare records we can only infer, basing on customs and deduce from partial archives.

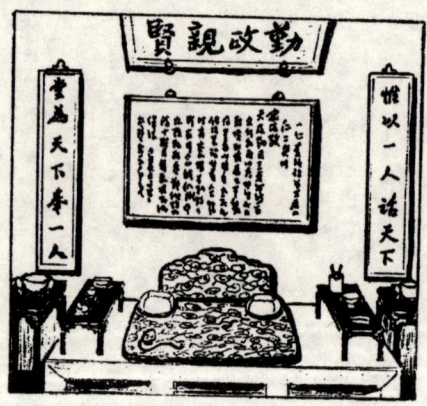

The side rooms of the rear building of *Yangxindian* are *Tishuntang* and *Yanxitang* where used to be the bedroom for the empress, of emperor Qianlong, Jiaqing and Daoguang. So the questions come out, wasn't *Kunninggong* the abode hall for the empress? Were not the 12 palaces for the imperial concubines including the empress? It is true that after the rebuilding in Qing dynasty the east room of *Kunninggong* had been used as the bridal chamber for the imperial couple, while the west spatial room was for sacrificing activities. It is also true that after wedding the empress would usually choose a courtyard of place among the 12 palaces, 6 in the east and 6 in the west. The Empress of the Emperor Xianfeng had lived in *Zhongcuigong* (Palace of Gathering Essence), the empress of emperor Tongzhi in *Chuxiugong* (Palace of Gathering Excellence), and the empress of Guangxu chose *Zhongcuigong* again for living. In other word, the palaces were used as the empress' residence, not that of the emperors. *Tishuntang* and *Yanxitang* were the places where the emperor lived together with his concubines besides his dropping in at their residences.

The outer envelope of the hall of *Yangxindian* has been called as the duty envelope. We cannot tell the original usage of the space unless we consult to Qing household archives of interior furnishings. According to the archives, wares and artifacts displayed in separate rooms of the envelope buildings were quite similar, which were mainly made of crystal and agate, though not as precious and gorgeous as those in high rank imperial concubines' rooms, obviously they were not for the maids or eunuchs. From an other point of view, taking into consideration the strict hierarchy system, maids' or eunuchs' duty rooms were not possible to be arranged so close to the emperor's bedroom in the rear yard. Now emerges our answer, the envelope was for the concubines of lower rank, such as *Guiren* and *Changzai* to serve the emperor.

As for the low inferior rows of buildings outside the Gate of Mental Cultivation, they were neither for imperial family members nor for the nobles and bodyguards whose rooms were of superior status and better conditions. As *Yangxindian* was the hall for the emperor to meet his ministers, to deal with state affairs and read over memorials to the throne, from the location and decoration grade, they were possibly the rooms for the eunuchs on duty, or the place for the officials to wait for the emperor's call.

42. Imperial Physician, a Fatal Job

There goes the old saying, *accompanying the emperor is no better than living with a tiger*. Risks were everywhere at every time when at the side of the monarch. Could it be worse if you were an imperial physician?

In the system of imperial palace the organization of the imperial physicians was called Taiyiyuan (Imperial Academy of Madicine) which is located outside the *Di'anmen* (Gate of Earthly Peace) to the north of imperial city. To be more convenient for service, the Zhulichu was set up as the resident physician department inside the Forbidden City. The chief official of Taiyiyuan was Yuanshi, the director of the court, and alike official setup in other organizations there were also two assistants. Physicians varied for their status, and the multitude of names include Taiyi (imperial physician), Limu (medical secretary) and Yishi (doctor). Every time a doctor went to see the special patient, he had to follow a eunuch from the imperial pharmacy. Every piece of prescription had to be cosigned by the physician, a eunuch and a pharmacist. Besides, every single medicament had to be made clear of its property, dosage and indication, cosigned again and submitted to the emperor, recorded in archives and used for future inspection or reference.

When herbs were decocted as required in Chinese medicine, the procedure had to be kept watch by an official from Taiyiyuan and a eunuch from the inner palace. When the medicine was done, it would be put into 2 cups, one to be tried by the physician and then the assistant official from Taiyiyuan, the other cup was for the emperor's use. If the procedure was not obeyed or any problem happened, all people involved would be punished for losing carefulness and respect, and if medicines were not efficient or were not able to save the emperor or in some extreme cases killed the emperor, fates of imperial physicians and relevant official are easy to foresee. When emperor Tongzhi died of smallpox, imperial physicians Li Deli and Zhuang Shouhe lost their rank and had to work as inferior labors for not doing their best to save the monarch. Several decades later when emperor Guangxu died of illness, another 3 doctors were removed from their position. Li Deli once wrote a prescription for the empress dowager Cixi, but unfortunately she could not go to sleep after taking the medicine and got bad temper. This caused chaos in the court, and also caused the physician be sent to the Ministry of

Punishment. Xu Fuchen who was a famous doctor in late Qing dynasty, watched every step inside the palace as if walking on thin ice. He looked after Cixi carefully but could not have time to save his daughter from the paw of death.

All the physicians from Taiyiyuan had the duty to look after the imperial concubines either of high ranks or inferior ones, and the cosigning and annotating regulations remained the same.

There were cases for the doctors to go out of the Forbidden City. Sometimes they would also go to see nobles or ministers when needed. Such home visits would be designated by the emperor, and all information including the illness and the reward given by the patient should be reported.

When the emperor went for a travel or inspection outside the Forbidden City, he would need physicians to escort him, either by his designation or on duty in turn.

43. Emperor's Calling in Ministers

In some films and literary works, the scene of the emperor's calling in his ministers is often deformed. It always depicts, the emperor sitting high on the throne, eunuchs and bodyguards standing on both sides. When the emperor whisper out his edict, the serving eunuch might claim, summon whoever to the hall, the voice would be repeated and enlarged one by one, and in hurry the official would come hastening to kneel down 3 times and kowtow 9 times. This is an imagination invented other than the reality recorded.

When Qing emperor summoned his ministers, he would not

sit on the throne in *Taihedian* (Hall of Great Harmony) as in grand ceremonies, but on the contrary, he would meet them in his private room near his bedroom. Ministers were usually called in after the emperor had his meal. Dishes were removed from the table, and the emperor would ask eunuchs to present a name list of the officials to meet. Posing himself on the *kang* (a heatable brick bed), he would then summon them in turns, and no eunuch was permitted to be on the site. The eunuch's task was to lead the ministers called in to wait in the duty room and then to go in for the meeting. He could reach no further than opening the portiere for the ministers and had to disappear from the view of the sovereign. Entering the room and saying "for your health, Your Majesty", the ministers knelt down and then stood up to sit on a mattress closer to the emperor. It was the time to report or answer the questions. Possibly the minister might be praised or blamed, and there were also rites for them. When praised and awarded, he was to kneel and kowtow again saying "thank Your Majesty", and when scolded he had to remove his official hat, kneel down and kowtow. Other than these 2 cases, ministers were not required to kowtow during meeting the lord. The meeting ended with the emperor's command "you can go back" or "you can pay respect now", thus the subordinate would stand up and kneel down to pay respect again, and then step backward facing the emperor to the door sill and turn to leave. This procedure is far simpler than that rendered by writers but must be obeyed strictly in those days.

44. Architectural Difference Between the East and West Six Palaces

On both sides of the three rear palaces on the middle axis are the east and west six courtyards of palaces where the imperial concubines lived. The names of the 12 complexes of palaces are *Jingrengong*, *Yanxigong*, *Chengqiangong*, *Yonghegong*, *Zhong-cuigong* and *Jingyanggong* in the east, and *Yongshougong*, *Taijidian*, *Yikungong*, *Changchungong*, *Chuxiugong* and *Xian-fugong* in the west. Largely symmetrically arranged, the structures of the courtyards of the east palace are different from that of the west. Should it not follow the law of symmetry in planning and building the Forbidden City? Why is the layout of the complexes in the east more tidy but rigid while that of the

west is more flexible?

Originally from the time when the Forbidden City was built in Ming dynasty to the late period of Qing dynasty, the layouts of these two areas were the same, strictly divided into courtyards of palaces, no single one purposely emphasized or degraded until the west six palaces were partially reconstructed at the end of Qing dynasty. It was the empress dowager Cixi who decided to change the layout of the west. Actually the reason of the decision originated from the fact that Cixi had lived in this area since she was selected into the palace as an imperial concubine of low status. In the 3rd month of the 6th year of emperor Xianfeng's reign, Cixi gave birth to a dragon son who was later emperor Tongzhi in *Chuxiugong* (Palace of Gathering Excellence) in the west. After the young emperor Tongzhi mounted the throne, Cixi was entitled as the Holy Mother Empress Dowager. She was also called as the West Empress Dowager for her residence inside the Forbidden City remained in the six west palaces. It is well-known that Cixi had seized the supreme power of the empire for 48 years, but there were some intervals among which was the time when emperor Tongzhi was old enough to rein. Cixi decided to move to live in *Changchungong* (Palace of Eternal Spring) at that time, and first thing she thought was to reconstruct the courtyard into a more pleasant place for leaving than the rigid layout under the hierarchy system as it was for such an extraordinarily eminent person as she was. She commanded the gate of *Changchungong* complex and the rear hall of *Taijidian* (Hall of Great Supremacy) to the south to be removed, and then to built a hall named *Tiyuandian* (Hall of State Unity) on the site, thus linking the two courtyards into one. Owning the two courtyards did not satisfy her, and so an opera stage was built at the back of *Tiyuandian*. It was called the theatrical stage of *Changchungong* (Palace of Eternal Spring) where had been a frequent resort for Cixi. At the same time, a similar reconstruction took place at the two courtyards of *Yikungong* (Palace of Blessings to Mother Earth) and *Chuxiugong*. A gate and a rear hall were removed and a linkage hall, *Tiyuandian*, was set up. Later to celebrate Cixi's 50th birthday in the 10th year of emperor Guangxu's reign, *Yikungong* and *Chuxiugong* were re-finished and painted. To make these 2 complexes the most gorgeous among all rear palaces it cost 630,000 taels of silver. Cixi then moved from *Changchungong* to *Chuxiugong*.

Although we still say that the rear palaces include the east six palaces and the six west palaces, the west part is not what had been according to the original design concept.

45. Emperor Wanli "Sojourn" in the West Palace

Largely speaking, *Qianqinggong* (Palace of Heavenly Purity) and *Yangxindian* (Hall of Mental Cultivation) were the formal offices for the emperors of Ming and Qing dynasties respectively, and the rear palaces in the east and west were for the imperial concubines. There was an emperor though who had lived and worked in *Qixiang* Palace, which was later called *Taijidian* (Hall of Great Supremacy), in the west six palaces, where the sojourn lasted decades. He was emperor Wanli of Ming dynasty, whose name was Zhu Yijun. Why did the eagle occupy the nest of a sparrow?

Most of Ming emperors lived in *Qianqinggong* and dealt with state affairs there in usual days. *Taijidian* was originally called *Weiyang* Palace at the early year of Ming dynasty. Since later emperor Jiajing's father who had not been the emperor himself was born in *Weiyang* Palace, Jiajing decided to change the name of the palace into *Qixiang* Palace that means the palace that brings auspiciousness. Emperor Wanli was born here too. But all these reasons cannot bring out the history that why the emperor had formally lived here for so long until the year of 1597, the 25th year of emperor Wanli's reign, when a big fire caused by lightning burned the front three halls and rear palaces including *Qianqing* Palace into ruin. Many of the important halls for ceremonies and working were damaged. The dynasty was on decline and the reconstruction could not be completed earlier than 1626, the 6th year of emperor Tianqi's reign. So during the long "homeless" period, emperor Tianqi had no choice but live in the *Qixiang* Palace where he was born. Though we can read in historical documents that some other emperors had lived in a rear palace for a rather long time, emperor Tianqi was the only emperor formally resided and worked in a palace prepared for the feminine.

In Qing dynasty, the name of *Qixiang* Palace was changed into *Taijidian*, which has a hexastyle facade and subtle interior screens of propitious creature motifs carved with Nan wood.

46. Imperial Concubine Zhen's Death

There is a very common well situated at a corner inside north gate of *Ningshougong* (Palace of Tranquility and Longevity) of the Forbidden City, which is the most famous "Zhen Fei Jing", Imperial Concubine Zhen Well.

Zhen Fei, imperial concubine Zhen, daughter of the minister of the Board of Rites in Qing dynasty, was the concubine of emperor Gungxu. She and her elder sister were selected at the same time into the imperial palace and she was granted the title of Zhen Pin and her sister as Jin Pin. Later in the year of Guangxu 21st (1895), she was promoted and granted the title as Zhen Fei. Zhen Fei was pretty and virtuous.

She liked poetry and was good at painting, and she was adept in performing musical instrument and singing, and was sanguine also. So she was deeply loved by Emperor Guangxu. Sometimes she was so bold to break free from conventions that she put on a gentleman's suit to act as an emperor or a eunuch. She accompanied Guangxu when he dealt with official affairs at *Yangxindian* (Hall of Mental Cultivation)

many times. Suffering constrained both in daily and political life, and suffering from depression, Guangxu was greatly comforted by Zhen Fei. In 1898, Zhen *Fei* supported the emperor to push the constitutional reform and modernization, thus put her on the political antithesis against Empress Dowager Cixi. She was arrested in a small courtyard to north of *Jingqige* by Cixi and was forbidden to meet the emperor since then.

There was another reason that aroused Cixi's hatred to Zhen Fei. While selecting the empress and concubines for Guangxu, Cixi forced Guangxu to chose her niece to be his empress, empress Longyu. Longyu was two years older than Guangxu and was not good looking too. Guangxu had no good impression on her and seldom contacted with her, but doted on Zhen Fei.

In the August of 1900 when the Eight Power Allied Forces invasion breached into Beijing, Cixi intended to seize Guangxu to flee to Xi'an and decided to kill Zhen Fei. Before the fleeing Cixi gave the command to the imperial chieftain eunuch Cui Yugui to take Zhen Fei out of her house. Having been arrested for long, the withered Zhen Fei knelt with trepidation at the foot of Cixi. At this time all the eunuchs served around were ordered to withdraw and keep off except Cui Yugui and Wang Dehuan. Cixi told Zhen Fei grimly, "The foreigners will breach into the city soon, in the turmoil and chaos of war if by any chance you are insulted, it would soil the imperial dignity and be a shame to our ancestor." Zhen Fei kowtow and said, "Your Grandma, you'd better stay away from the capital for the time being, the emperor has to assume emperor's command at the imperial capital to make vigorous efforts to struggle against the critical peril." Cixi sneered and reprimanded, "You will be killed immediately, how dare you to speak like that." She then pointed to the well in the yard and said, "bestow the death to you, take her away". Zhen Fei supplicated, "Your Grandma, I beg you to let your slave meet the emperor at the last." "You just absurdly hoped that the emperor shield you, go away to die", answer Cixi. At this moment, Cui Yugui moved the cover away from the well. Zhen Fei choked with sobs and her face bathed in tears, "The death of your slave is worthless, but how about the imperial power of our Qing dynasty". Not until she finished her saying Cixi ordered Cui Yugui loudly, "push her down into the well". Zhen Fei was dragged up and forced into the well with her grievous crying voice. Then the well was covered. Zhen Fei was 25 years old at that time. Her body was salvaged out from the well a year later. In commemoration of Zhen Fei, her sister set up a small mourning hall in a small room to the north of that well, namely *"Huaiyuantang"*. And that well was called Zhen Fei well since then.

47. How was the Latest Emperor Forced to Leave the Forbidden City?

Empress dowager Longyu promulgated the imperial edict for the abdication of the emperor of Qing dynasty on Feb. the 12th, 1912, thus ended the 268 years ruling of Qing dynasty. It was announced at the same time that the imperial system was perished in China forever. According to the terms of preferential treatment for the abdicated Qing imperial family though, the members of the family could live in the rear part of the Forbidden City after the emperor's abdication and remain their honorific title. From 1912 till 1924, there were emperor and courtier, and imperial robe and court wears remained the same, as if nothing had being changed. The abdicated emperor Puyi and the imperial family still lived in their small royal court.

General Feng Yuxiang staged the Beijing Coup in 1924 and decided to expel the last emperor out of the palace and to amend the terms of preferential treatment for abdicated Qing imperial family. The major contents of such amendment include abrogating the honorific title of Qing emperor, removing imperial family from the Forbidden City immediately to other place and etc. The amended terms of preferential treatment for the abdicated Qing imperial family was passed by the governors on Nov. 4th the same year. The commander in chief, general Lu

Zhonglin, and police chief inspector Zhang Bi was ordered to accompany a social noted personage Li Yuying to go to execute at the Forbidden City.

In the morning of Nov. 5th, Lu Zhonglin, Zhang Bi and Li Yuying led less than a hundred soldiers and police men to the Forbidden City. They cut off the telephone line which connect the palace with the outside at first, and then marched into the north gate. They set up guards at each gate they passed. Lu Zhonglin and the others went to Puyi's living place directly, where Puyi had just had his fruit dishes and was chatting with Wanrong in *Chuxiugong* (Palce of Gathering Excellence). The emperor sent Shaoying, minister of Household Affairs, to negotiate the outcomers. When Shaoying knew the amended terms of preferential treatment for the abdicated Qing imperial family and Puyi was required to leave the palace immediately, he was stupefied, but pretend be calm and censured that the Republic Government contradicted the previous preferential treatment terms for the imperial family. Lu Zonglin pointed out solemnly, "you have to understand we came here to execute the order of state council, we are responsible for the Republic of China and for the abdicated Qing dynasty. If there were others here but not us, you wouldn't be so unrushed. No further discussion now!" Lu Zhonglin gave the order right away that Puyi and his followers had to move out from Forbidden City within 3 hours. But the grand concubine dowagers Jingyu and Ronghui refused to move out persistently. Through negotiations, it was finally agreed that the moving could be delayed no later than 3 p. m. But at 3 : 30 p. m., Puyi and the others still wanted to stall for time further. When this was noticed by Lu Zhonglin, he told his suite loudly on purposed, "Hurry up, tell the surrounding troop although time is due, we will still negotiate, don't fire the cannon at the moment, waiting for another 20 minutes". Puyi turned pale with fright when he heard that and agreed to move out immediately from the imperial palace. Hastily, Puyi and his royal family left the Forbidden City where they had prolonged the occupation for 12 years after abdicating.

48. Imperial Garden— the Wander Land

Imperial Garden of the Forbidden City is unique for its exquisiteness and solemnity. The garden is linked with the rear palaces in middle route, the east part and the west part. It had been used as a place for amusement for the imperial family. There are many potted landscapes and rockery works decorated among the ancient cypress trees and Chinese scholar trees. Pavilions, terraces, temples and gates are arranged on a symmetrical plan, and the pavement on the plan is embroidered with fine pebble inlays. Contrary to Chinese gardens that reflect typical Chinese philosophy of nature, Imperial Garden in the Forbidden City gives a much clearer sense of a rear garden along the main axis of the palace. Buildings inside the garden mainly include *Qin'andian* (Hall of Imperial Peace), *Yangxingzhai* (Studio of Character Cultivation), *Jiangxuexuan* (Pavilion of Crimson Snow), *Chizaotang* (Hall of Literary Elegance), *Yanhuige* (Pavilion of Extending Sunshine), a pair of pavilions and a grand rockery.

At the center of the garden is *Qin'andian*, a Daoist temple, enveloped with a square wall. Three statues of Daoist Gods are consecrated inside. It was believed that the gods could control natural power, so they were worshiped to save the imperial palace from fire or other disasters.

Yangxingzhai is located in the southwest corner of the garden. After the last emperor Puyi abdicated, he learned English and mathematics in this tow-story building.

Jiangxuexuan is opposite to *Yangxingzhai*. It is in the south east corner facing westward. There were 5 Chinese flowering crabapple trees in front of the building. Every time they blossomed, petals swirled in the air, as if it was snowing with crimson flakes. The name of the building was the idea of emperor Qianlong. Later when empress dowager Cixi ruled the country, she asked to plant peace flowers to take place of the crabapples. Gone the trees, gone the petals, and gone the poetic imagination.

Chizaotang, as the name indicates, was the place for the emperor to store his book collection and to read in his spare time. The hall is situated to the north of *Jiangxuexuan* in the northeast corner of the garden.

Yanhuige is another two-story building in the west part

garden at the foot of the north wall. Emperor Qianlong, Daoguang and Xianfeng all enjoyed this building very much and often came here to write poems. Besides this, the building had also been used for selecting imperial maids for the emperor.

Wanchunting and *Qianqiuting*, literarily the Pavilion of Ten Thousand Springs and the Pavilion of Thousand Autumns, are a couple of pavilions that are same in shape, scale and decoration, and are symmetrically located.

A grand rockery works is located symmetrical to the building of *Yanhuige*. Rocks of rare shapes are composed together to make a micro mountain world. In the middle on the bottom, there is a cave inside a tunnel entrance. On each hand on the tunnel there is a dragon fountain which can spray water upward. A left path and a right path lead to the top of the mountain where the Pavilion of Imperial Views is located. In Qing dynasty, during festival of the 7th day of the 7th lunar month, emperor would bring his family to give offering to the spirits of the Cowherd and the Girl Weaver, and during the night of Mid-autumn Festival, the imperial family would also come here to enjoy the moonlight, and moreover, when the Double Ninth Festival (9th day of the 9th lunar month) came, these people would be on the top of the mountain to share the distant view.

There are 3 pieces of the rarest stones displayed inside the garden. One is famous for its vein that looks like the image of Kongming prostrating to the Big Dipper. Kongming was a most intelligent military strategist in the 3rd century. Both the stories of Kongming and the stone of his image are deeply loved by Chinese people. Another stone has a strange shape, as if it were composed of hundreds of sea cucumbers. These 2 pieces are near each other. The 3rd piece is a timber fossil. Emperor Qianlong had written a poem for it and carved it in a flat surface of the fossil. It is placed in front of *Jiangxuexuan* (Pavilion of Crimson Snow).

Pebble pavement is another characteristic of the garden. There are altogether more than 900 patterns and many stories from historic novels and folk tales.

49. Theatrical Stages in the Forbidden City

In the Forbidden City, there are five stages that are all suitable for different performances. They are respectively the large theatrical stage of *Changyin'ge* (Pavilion of Pleasant Sound), the stage of *Shufangzhai* (Lodge of Fresh Fragrance), the stage of *Changchungong* (Palace of Eternal Spring) and other two small ones—the stage of *Juanqinzhai* (Lodge for Retired Life) and the stage named *Fengyacun* (Preservation of Elegance) in the Lodge of Fresh Fragrance.

The stage of *Changyin'ge*, built in Qianlong's reign, facing to the south, is the largest stage in the Forbidden City. It consists of three stages successively from top to bottom called Futai (Stage of Happiness), Lutai (Stage of Good Fortune) and Shoutai (Stage of Longevity). The lower stage or the Longevity Stage is most spacious. In the center of it, there is a well used for drawing water and producing the resounding effect according to the needs of performances. When moving the stage board, a throughway leading to the backstage can be found. In addition, there is a windlass (capstan) fixed on the Happiness Stage and openings in the ceilings of the stages, through which actors could play some grand scenes when performing such traditional operas as "The Monkey King Causing Havoc in Heaven" or "Eight Immortals Crossing the Sea" and so forth. Opposite *Changyin'ge* is *Yueshilou* (Building for Watching Performance), a two-storied building where the emperor and his empress and concubines would enjoy operas.

The stage of *Shufangzhai*, with a double-eaved roof, is the second in the court. Though a single-storied stage, it's spacious enough for ordinary opera to perform. During the abdicated emperor Puyi's time, the well-known Beijing Opera actors Mei Lanfang, Jiang Miaoxiang and others were once asked to act the traditional operas here.

Another stage, standing in the yard of *Changchungong*, was built after *Changchunmen* (Eternal Spring Gate) and the rear hall of *Taijidian* (Hall of Great Supremacy) was demolished at the time when the six western palaces were renovated in the late Qing Dynasty. The Empress Dowager Cixi, on the occasion of celebrating her 50th birthday, once enjoyed traditional operas with concubines and ministers' spouses here for 15 days.

Besides the opened stages above mentioned, there are still two elegant smaller indoor stages respectively in *Juanqinzhai* (Lodge for Retired Life) and *Shufangzhai* (Lodge of Fresh Fragrance), which were mainly used for the purpose of the emperor, his empress, and concubines to watch Chinese traditional operas on their own.

In the early days, the operas performed in the court were mostly *Kunqu* opera, *Yiyangqiang* opera and other local popular tunes. By the late Qing period, though, the Beijing Opera was more commonly put on instead. Beside the regular theatrical troupe, eunuchs who had learned singing and acting operas in the court also gave performances sometimes.

50. The Western Music Introduced into the Imperial Court

In some films, TV plays and literary works the image of and descriptions about the last Qing Emperor Puyi in western-style clothes or enjoying western music could be easily watched and read. Actually, more than two hundred years before that time, or as early as the emperor Kangxi's reign, the western music had already been introduced into the Forbidden City. During the period of Qianlong, even a symphony orchestra beginning to take shape was once set up in the imperial court.

The Qing Emperor Kangxi had great musical attainments and was also very interested in western music. At that time, the

western missionaries who served in the Qing court, such as Ferdinand, Thomas Pereira and others not only tributed western music instruments to the Emperor Kangxi, but also showed him how to play them. In the mean time they also passed on him some music theories. In his letter submitted to the King of Luise XIV, the French missionary Bai Jin (Joachim bouvet) wrote, "Emperor Kangxi likes the western musical instruments and musical theories very much, and is interested in playing them as well. If only he makes some practices in his leisure time, he can play the western instruments as well as he plays most Chinese and Dadan musical instruments". At that time though, the western music was yet to be regarded as the personal entertainment of the Emperor Kangxi himself. By the Qianlong's reign, a western orchestra was really founded in the Qing Court.

Although there are no special written records about this orchestra, we can still learn a rough state from some fragmentary materials in the archives of the Qing court. The related records read as follows: "In 1742 (the 7th year of Emperor Qianlong's reign), eunuch Gao Yu and others handed in one *pipa* (a plucked string instrument); six *sanxian* (a three-stringed plucked instrument); ten small *laqin* (music instrument); one long *laqin* (music instrument); eight western flutes; three bamboo clappers, and one *sheng* (a reed pipe wind instrument). Delivering the imperial order: westerners will be summoned to come into the court and recognize these instruments. In the meanwhile, young eunuchs in the Inner Court were ordered to learn from those who were skilled in playing these instruments. " According to another record in the Qing archives, the iron-wire Qin was once made in the Qing court. In addition, "following the imperial order in 14th year of Qianlong's reign (1749) ···fourteen suits of clothes for western musicians should be made, but the fashion drafts should be submitted before sewing began."

From the scattered materials mentioned above, we can hold that these musical instruments once recognized and taught by westerners must be western ones. Among them *Pipa*, *Sanxian* may be guitar and mandolin; long *laqin* and small *laqin* are probably violoncello and violin; western flute may belong to the Eustachian tube, or some kind of clarinet; the iron-wire *qin* is ought to be the harp or piano. Furthermore, on the basis of the imperial order of making costumes for western musicians, we can reasonably conclude that no matter who are meant by the "western musicians", the westerners or the eunuchs of the inner court who played the western music instruments, anyway, it's no doubt, there really was a western orchestra of 14 members in the imperial court. It would be a small-scale orchestra that gave the main instrumental performances of indoor light music.

51. Spirit Motifs on Stone Carving in Front of *Qin'andian*

In the ancient times, on account of the lack of scientific knowledge of the nature, people were likely to explain natural phenomena and laws as the power of gods. Praying to the gods had been regarded as the only way to get rid of misfortunes and disasters. Superstitious activities in the Forbidden City had many varieties beyond our imagination. No doubt that the last emperor Puyi wrote in his reminiscence *My Early Years*, if all superstitious activities were collected, the record must be thicker than the book *Liao Zhai* (*Chat about Tales*). That had been the fact. Regarded as the son of the Heaven by others and himself, emperors were not so confident about their power of controlling the fate unless he had got blessing and protection of the gods. That is why many temples of different believe systems were built in the Forbidden City, and all kinds of gods within reach were enshrined and worshipped.

Among the spirits and gods worshipped in the Forbidden City, the Daoist God was one of the most fortunate who can enjoy the offerings every now and then. It was said that during emperor Jiajing's reign in Ming dynasty, *Qin'andian* (Hall of Imperial Peace) caught a fire. It was the Daoist God Zhenwu who led his army of water spirits, put out the fire and saved the building.

People say that the footprints on the step at the northeast stair were left by Zhenwu when he was concentrating on fighting with the fire. Nobody knows whether the footprints were carved by the eunuchs or whatever, but the story survived hundreds of years. All the participants of the fighting, including sea monster, fish, shrimp, crab and other water creatures, thus, had their position on flag post stone in front of *Qin'andian* where was regarded as an important place along the middle axis. It shows that there was some kind of exceptional treatment to such creatures and spirits, which reflects strongly the desire for favorable rains and the wishes for the peace of the palace buildings.

52. The Dragon Fountain at the Foot of the Grand Rockery

Looking from the north gate of the Forbidden City, we can see only two buildings above the high red wall, one is the two-story building *Yanchunge* (Pavilion of Extending Sunshine), and the other is *Yujingting* (Pavilion of the Imperial Views).

Before the middle of the Ming dynasty, there had been a Hall of Appreciating Flowers, and during emperor Wanli's reign, a composition of rockery works was built on the site. Composed with so many pieces of rare rocks, this works has the largest scale of all the rockeries inside the Forbidden City. In front of the grand rockery is a pair of stone pedestals of lions. Inside the basin on the each pedestal is a stone carved dragon facing up to the sky. When it works, water is to be sprayed out from the dragon's mouth.

Is the water resource natural or manmade? Beijing did not have strong spring resources in Ming and Qing dynasties nor today, if it were not manmade water pressure, the fountain would not work. All the spraying water we see today is run by two giant water vats placed on the top of the rockery works and the pipe lines linking the vats and the fountains below.

Not only the fountains, but also the water channels where wine cups floats are also run by such devices. Though initially, these water plays worked well in history, since the pipes are made of copper, they are likely to rust, so all the devices had to be maintained every now and then.

53. Qianlong Garden, an Exotic Flower in the History of Chinese Gardening

Qianlong Garden is a part of *Ningshougong* (Palace of Longevity and Tranquility) precinct, so its formal name is *Ningshougong* Garden. The building complex of *Ningshougong* was built for emperor Qianlong's retired life after reining the empire for 60 years. He named many of the buildings himself, which reflects deeply his thoughts. For example, *Suichutang*, the Hall of Fulfilling Original Wishes, indicates to his promise that he would not rein longer than his grandfather emperor Kangxi who had been the sovereign for 61 year, and *Juanqinzhai*, literarily the Lodge of Tired of Diligence, can be referred to the

short form as the Lodge of Retirement, gives out clearly his diligence of being a monarch and his will for a rest after the long reign.

The garden is most famous for its layout and exquisite arrangement of the buildings. Actually the site of the garden was not perfect for buildings and creating sceneries, which is 160 meters long and 37 meters wide. Such a narrow site presented tough questions and unexpectedly a chance for the architects and gardeners to give a full play to their talents, skills and wisdom. Not only this restriction was overcome by the garden designer, but also was taken advantage of by merging together different styles of gardening, southern and northern. The unique coordination of the master styles shows brilliant concepts and supreme gardening skills. Thus the eminent works came into being, as commented, "suits well, delicate and fashionable".

The garden was divided into 4 successive quadrangle yards of 4 specific flavors.

There is a rockery work right inside the gate of the first courtyard, hiding the inner scene. A small tortuous path was applied according traditional method of laying gardens, leading to the main pavilion of the yard at the visional center, *Guhuaxuan* (Pavilion of Ancient Glory) that was named after an ancient Chinese catalpa tree. Nothing but screens of casements were used in the pavilion to form a flexible space of the exterior and the interior. No egos but a feeling of unity of nature and being can be comprehended. To the southwest of the pavilion, facing the rockeries and platform in the east, is *Xishangting* (Pavilion for Enjoying Drinking), containing a mini canal where wine cups once had been floating on running water, and where poems had been floating from acute minds, alluding the story that the most famous ancient calligrapher Wang Xizhi once depicted in his master work *Lantingxu* (Prelude for the Orchid Pavilion Poem). Upper on the hill north to the pavilion, *Xuhuiting* (Chamber of the Morning Sun) was built facing the east, while a small garden with a pavilion called *Xiefangting* (Pavilion of Gethering the Fragrance) enveloped by verandas was arranged in the southeast corner of the first courtyard.

Behind *Guhuaxuan*, a flora-pendant gate stands and opens to the second courtyard of vernacular residential style, plain and amiable. Decorated by spots of rockery works, the main hall of the yard, *Suichutang* (Hall of Fulfilling Original Wishes), was situated in the back on the axis, manifesting Qianlong's vow and fulfilling of the 60 years of reign.

The third yard, a hidden and astonishing scene, was composed of compact rockeries. A pavilion (Pavilion of Lofty Beauty) on the top of the hill overlooking the entire layout, caves, stone steps and verandas link the separated buildings, *Cuishanglou* (Tower for Viewing Beautiful Scenery), *Yanqulou* (Tower for Prolonging Taste) and *Sanyouxuan* (Three Friends Lodge). Interior works of the buildings are fantastic among which that in *Sanyouxuan* specially designed on screens and furniture, the characters of pine, bamboo and plum blossom have the nature of facing the snow, metaphorically representing 3 human qualities. Together with pine, bamboo and plum planted outside the chamber, Emperor Qianlong showed off his tastes and merits.

The fourth yard was designed after *Jianfugong* Garden, a Qianlong's favorite garden in the Forbidden City built in the early period of his reign.

In the center *Fuwangge* (Pavilion of the Anticipation of Good Fortune) is located and is style in a hexastyle elevation in four directions, square in plan and double-eaved on facade, imitating *Yanchunge* (Building for Prolonging Spring). With a pyramidical roof, *Fuwangge* is the highest building in Qianlong Garden. The building is accompanied by a little pavilion on the rockery of plum motifs and of a plan shaped as a plum blossom, *Biluoting* (Pavilion of Green Spiral Shell). The little pavilion was designed to partially imitate a square pavilion (Pavilion of Piling Emeralds) in *Jianfugong* Garden.

Surrounding *Fuwangge*, a L-shaped *Yunguanglou* (Building of Cloud Light) is situated in the southeast, and *Yucuixuan*

(Pavilion of Jade and Emerald) in the east, and *Juanqinzha*i (Lodge for Retired Life) that was aimed to imitate *Jingsheng-zhai*, a lodge in *Jianfugong* Garden, is the rear row of the yard at the north. Through the verandas, people can access all the buildings from *Fuwangge*. To the west of *Juanqinzhai*, inside the octagonal gate and in the shade of bamboos, is *Zhuxiangguan* (Room of Bamboo Fragrant), that is also linked with the Lodge through verandas.

Ningshougong Garden is compact and contains changing vistas, for the 4 courtyards were designed according to 4 concepts. In order to form identical scenes and theatrical effects, the architects applied architectural environmental vocabularies of verandas flat and sloped, paths contouring and hunching, plants of various kinds, and rockery works forming caves and bridges, which interact together with the multiple building forms up on the hills and behind other elements, so as to block the view of the surrounding walls. Also by means of using other parts of the palace axis as a background, the garden was of rich and colorful views.

54. *Ci'ninggong* and its Garden

　　As the old saying goes, the emperor had 3 palaces and 6 courtyards for his 72 concubines. Though the counting was not precise, it reflects the fact that the emperors used to have a large family. What would it bring if the old emperor was gone and the successor mounted the throne? The answer is that all the empress dowagers had to move out from the palaces they occupied to the courtyards for the widows.

　　Ci'ninggong (Palace of Compassion and Tranquility) is located outside the inner forbidden gate, *Longzongmen*, in the west of the Forbidden City. This building complex was built in

Ming dynasty, and repaired in the Qing dynasty. The complex is composed of several courtyards and buildings, including the main courtyard of *Ci'ninggong*, the Garden of *Ci'ninggong*, the courtyard of *Shoukanggong* (Palace of Longevity and Well-Being), *Shou'an'gong* (Palace of Longevity and Tranquility) and the Buddhist temple of *Yinghuadian* (Hall of Exuberance).

Guarded with two majestic-looking bronze kylins, the main courtyard of *Ci'ninggong* shows its solemnness and significance. The *Ci'ninggong* was for the previous empress, and the other smaller courtyards were allotted to subordinate dowagers.

The low ranking dowager's treatment was far from that of the higher ranking dowager. The empress dowager received the most luxurious services of them all. There are some stories of the unfortunate ladies who had been neglected when the master was alive and led an even more desolated life than to be a widow. In some cases, they could not get enough daily necessities. They had no choice but doing some sewing and asking eunuchs to bring it out for some money.

Dowagers were not allowed to leave their palaces, their only relief was the *Buddhist world*, and their only pleasure might be the times in the Garden of *Ci'ninggong* which was built in Ming dynasty, and covers a land of 6,400 square meters.

Unlike most Chinese gardens of free plan, *Ci'ninggong* Garden has a symmetrical layout, which is neither gorgeously decorated as the Imperial Garden nor delicately arranged as the Qianlong Garden. The all elements used in gardens include a Buddhist Hall, some two-story buildings, a pavilion, 2 small and cozy courtyards, a little water surface and some rockery works. Most of the buildings were for religious purposes, and emperor Qianlong had been living in one of the courtyards to decoct medical herbs for his mother who lived in the other courtyard to the opposite.

55. The Last Great Fire During the Last Emperor's Residence

Most of the Chinese ancient buildings were timber structured. Owing to the lack of scientific fire protecting measures and suitable equipment to extinguish fires, fire disasters were occurring in the Forbidden City's history frequently. In Ming and Qing dynasties only the three main halls of the Forbidden City had been burned for six times. Most of these fire were caused by thunder and seldom by the negligence, but the cause of the conflagration occurred in the abdicated Qing period was get uncovered till now.

Empress dowager Longyu promulgated the imperial edict for the abdication on Feb. the 12th of 1912, thus ended the 268 years ruling of Qing dynasty. According to the terms of preferential treatment for the abdicated Qing imperial family, the last emperor Puyi could live in the rear part of the Forbidden City after the abdication, and honorable titles of the imperial family were remained; therefore the abdicated Puyi still lived in his small royal life.

In the night of 26th June 1923 *Jianfugong* (Palace of Establishing Happiness) Garden, which is located at northwest corner of the Forbidden City, suddenly caught on fire. The fire started from the *De'rixindian* and spreaded quickly to *Yanchun-*

ge, *Jingyixuan*, *Guangshenlou*, *Zhongzhengdian*, *Xiangyunting* and many other buildings. In a moment the flames lit up the sky, billowing smoke and raging flames burned the entire night and was put out in the morning of the next day.

Jianfugong Garden was one of the four gardens in the emperor's palace. There were pavilions, platforms, buildings, and lofts connected one by others. The flowery winding corridors crisscrossed and meandered in the garden. There were lots of gold statues of Buddha, gold pagodas, gold ritual implements, and Tibetan Buddhist sutra enshrined in those buildings. The portraits of nine emperors of the Qing dynasty, sketches of imperial leisure life, antiques and famous treasured paintings had been stored there also. All the presents of Puyi's wedding ceremony were there too, so it was the place where a great part of the collection of treasures among the most valuable collections was gathered. After the fire, numerous treasures and the buildings of *Jianfugong* Garden vanished to ashes.

According to the report to Puyi from minister of Imperial Household Department, after the *Jianfugong* conflagration 508 bags of melted golden statues and ashes of Buddhist sutra and 43 boxes of fragmentary jade articles had been gathered, while they were clearing away the burned dilapidated ruins.

The reason that caused the *Jianfugong* conflagration was not yet discovered until today, and there were many conjectures. One of which stales that it might have been caused from careless use of lighting candles in the niche of Buddha. Another stales that because of the lack of electric knowledge and improper management, an electric fire occurred, but Puyi deemed that the eunuchs of that area who had stolen things wanted to disguise their guilt by intentionally committing arson. There has been no evidence that has supported any of those inferences yet. No one knows when this mysterious cause of the fierce and brutal fire could be brought to the light.

56. Stories of the Archery Pavilion

In the south of the square outside *Jingyunmen* (Gate of Great Fortune) stands a building alone of dignity and pride. The building has glazed roof of *Xieshan* style which refers to the style of four slopes plus two gables at both sides. The name of the building Archery Pavilion does not quite match its appearance. It is a grand hall in scale and style other than a pavilion.

The Archery Pavilion was originally built in Qing dynasty which was established by people of Manchu. This simple statement covers long and rich stories. The race of Manchu originated from the regions northeast of China of wild and vast land along mountains and rivers. Ancestors of Manchu lived by hunting, fishing and gathering. Skills of equestrian and archery did not only provide basic living but also trained agile and brave cavalry units of the Eight Banners. Relying on the troops, Manchu defeated Ming dynasty, set up then stabilized the dynasty of Qing. Qianlong period was in the mid of the dynasty when the state was peaceful and prosperous; thus the empire entered a flourishing age. Peaceful years and achievements brought pride and luxury among the Manchu nobles, equestrian and archery skills became yesterday memories and no more prevailed. Many Manchu customs had been lost and that of Han nationality were more and more popularized. A great number of Manchu offspring became even more proud of being able to have good command of the Chinese language, to write Chinese traditions poems and to be fellows of Chinese scholars. Emperor Qianlong worried about this situation and tendency and thought traditional Manchu culture was facing the dangers of extinction and Manchu's rule was to be threatened. So came out the imperial edict, summoned princes, dukes and officials to review the ancestor's edicts on the 20th of the 3rd lunar month of the 17th year of Qianlong period, saying that Manchu customs and traditions must be remembered and followed. The Archery Pavilion was repaired at that time to manifest the emperor's determination. Aside from this, a stele was erected inside the pavilion on which Qianlong's writing of the proclamation was carved. Some of the edict reads, "Clothes and language both should follow that of the tradition", "Drillings and demonstration, equestrian and archery, be constantly exercised", and "our later generations from Eight Banner must firstly be engaged in Manchu language and military skills, those who are proficient will be employed by the state regardless of their education in Chinese literature".

Another important reason of Qianlong's repairment of the Archery Pavilion may lie in the fact that he himself deeply love equestrian and archery. He was a master of riding horses and had learned archery from an expert shooter, duke Yunxi. It was said that once during a hunting when bodyguards drew a bear into the range of shooting, the bear suddenly was infuriated and sprung onto the hunters. Emperor Qianlong calmly mounted his horse and shot arrows at it. With help of his bodyguards, the emperor killed the bear and gained reputation for his bravery.

After the repair works in Qianlong period, emperors including Qianlong and Jiaqing had exercised shooting and other martial arts at the Archery Pavilion. Every time when drillings were on, the emperor and his boys would ride horses and shoot arrows in the square, or with the doors open and stand in the pavilion and aim at targets outside. There were also guards standing around the building and beating drums to cheer for the shooters.

57. Architectural Characteristics of *Wenyuan'ge*

There is a two-story building of black glazed tiled roof with green rim located in the east part of the front court area of the Forbidden City. Its tile works and style is unique in many of the splendid buildings in the imperial palace complex. The building is called *Wenyuan'ge* (Pavilion of Source of Literature). Its characteristics are reflected not only on its typical building style and decoration, but also on its history of having been the place for storing the greatest series of books and the greatest reference books, *Si Ku Quan Shu* (*the Complete Library in Four Divisions*) and *Gujin Tushu Jicheng* (*the Collection of Ancient and Modern Books*).

Wenyuan'ge was originally built during emperor Qianlong's reign, and was dedicated to storing the great volumes. *Si Ku Quan Shu (the Complete Library in Four Divisions)* is the greatest series of book in China's history. The four indexes are canon, history, treatise, and miscellany. The series has almost 80,000 volumes organized into 36,300 books. It took more than 10 year from the 37th to the 47th year of Qianlong period to complete.

Two years after the work of compiling the great volumes (1774), the emperor commanded to build *Wenyuan'ge* to the north of *Wenhuadian* (Hall of Literary Glory) to store the books after completion.

Wenyuan'ge was built after a most famous library, *Tianyige* in Ningbo of Zhejiang province. The building has 5 main bays on the facade, and plus the staircase forms a hept-style elevation. There is a structural floor between the 2 functional floors. The roof structure is *Xieshan* style and covered by black glazed tiles with green verges. The color arrangement applied Chinese traditional philosophy of the feminine and the masculine and the though of five basic elements in nature. Each of the five basic elements has a directional position and takes on a designated color, and black is the color for water. Odd numbers are masculine, while even numbers are feminine. As it is noted in the Book of Changes, the number 6 stands for water, a feminine element in this sense. Aside from this, patterns of water and dragon are used on glazed ridge tiles, sea horses are painted on beams, pillars are painted green, and water animals are carved on stone balustrades. It was a common belief then that invaluable books could thus be protected. In front of the building there is a pool upon which lies a stone bridge, and a stele pavilion is also standing to the east of the building. The stele shows Emperor Qianlong's writing on why and how *Wenyuan'ge* was built. The works of *the Complete Literary in Four Divisions* had been stored in boxes made of *Nan* wood on the shelves, and catalogued clearly.

There have been 7 copies of *the Complete Literary in Four devisions*, another 3 stored in Imperial libraries within the reach of the inner court, including *Wenjin'ge* in Chengde, *Wenshuoge* in Shenyang, *Wenyuan'ge* in Summer Palace of Yuanmingyuan, the other 3 in local libraries in southern China, namely *Wenhuige* in Yangzhou, *Wenzongge* in Zhenjiang and *Wenlan'ge* in Hangzhou.

58. Stories of the Nine-Dragon Screen

Nine-Dragon Screen is well known as a treasure of Chinese architecture. Only 3 screens of this kind remain in China, one was built in Ming dynasty in Datong of Shanxi province, and the other is located in Beihai Park during emperor Qianlong's reign. The Nine-Dragon Screen in the Forbidden City is most delicately carved and glazed and most representative in artistic characteristics. It came to the world in the year of 1771, the 36th year of Qianlong period when *Ningshougong* precinct was reconstructed.

The Nine-Dragon Screen in the Forbidden City is facing the north on the south enclosure wall of *Ningshougong* precinct. The

screen and *Huangjimen* (Gate of Imperial Supremacy) together identify the space that indicates the beginning of the building complex. The roof is covered with yellow glazed tiles, and the pedestal is made of carved white stone in Sumeru style. The body, the most expressive of all, is composed of 270 pieces of glazed bricks. Sea wave forms the general background, above which are 9 dragons of different colors roaring and tossing in the rolling sea. "9" as the paramount number for the imperial, 9 dragons stand for the most superior status of all screens. Yellow, as the imperial color, is applied to the dragon in the middle, and other colors, blue, purple and white of the dragons are selected and arranged together to accompany the yellow. Every detail of the dragons, tooth, hair, scale, paw and eyeball, is delicately carved, and the glazed surface is shining in the sunlight. In general, Nine-Dragon Screen has deep cultural implication, most representative artistic motifs, and strong expressive material and craftsmanship. It vividly reflects and narrates imperial culture of the Qing dynasty.

When the screen was built, components of precise size and building skills of the highest level were required. The size of each piece of glazed brick was extraordinary, and colors and curves of every piece were to match perfectly with each other. It was necessary to make 3 or 4 pieces for each individual component in case of damage, color change or deformation in kiln, and damage or repair when built.

Dragon, a composition of characters of life creatures, is a conceptual figure of Chinese people. It has the head of lion or tiger, the body of python, the scale of fish, the paw of crocodile.

Depicted by craftsmen and worshipped by emperors, dragon has been regarded as the symbol of Chinese nationalities, and Chinese people is thought to be the carriers of the story and spirit of dragon. In the long history of China, the totem of dragon is a most significant role. It would be impossible if the screen had not used the motif of dragon.

After more than 200 years of changes of weather and of the world, the screen of nine dragons has not changed much, shining brightly and lustrously, silently and steadily. It is a crystallization of the wisdoms, skills, and beliefs of ancient Chinese people.

59. Drainage System of
the Forbidden City

The Forbidden City, composed of more than 90 courtyards, covers an area of 720,000 square meters. In the rainy seasons of Beijing, how could the rainwater be conducted out of the city? It is a hidden question but fatally practical. Both, the question and the answer was brewed and solved by the designers of the Forbidden City, a successful drainage system was constructed when the complex of imperial palaces were built.

The drainage system in the Forbidden City adopts both devices underground and on the ground . In grand courtyards of

most significant buildings as the front three halls and rear three palaces, open drains are used. On the platforms of buildings a carefully designed slight slope lets water drain into the ditches. An interesting example is the triple platform of the front three halls where carved stone balustrades were built. On the groundsills the decorated water outlets are made. Most remarkably, 1,142 dragonhead waterspouts stretching out from each level of the base are arranged rhythmically, and the sight would be unmatchably grandiose when water is sprayed from the mouths of the dragons during heavy rains. All the rainwater is collected by the open drain around the bases of the enclosure buildings, and then, will be led to pass the small tunnels on the stairs and bases to reach the inner golden river.

What we cannot see but no less moving is the underground devices. It yet can be infer from the stone board covers along the streets and paths inside the city. For example, the path paved with stone all the way from the east to the west inside the north gate. Under the stone pavement is a most important main drain that conducts water to upper reach of the inner golden river in the northwest. Another main drain connected with this one is from the northeast corner of the Forbidden City to the lower reach of the river in the southeast, passing some subordinate buildings of the city. There are also branches, sub-branches and etc., woven together delicately and complicatedly. Most of drains are still in function today that the Palace Museum relies on to keep the city from rainwater deposit. Along the streets separating the east and west six palaces, in the squares in the buildings, sub-branches conduct water into the branches and branches into the main drains, and also in some cases, the line is linked with a small pond, and with other source of water supply, the drain helps when the pond needs to be emptied and refilled. Since the ground level is higher in the north and lower in the south at almost 2 meters in the Forbidden City, it brought about even tougher tasks to the designers of the original system, but the effectiveness and efficiency have been proved to be successful.

After 500 years, the drainage system in the Forbidden City has undergone the trials of thousands of heavy rains. People in history and today are another factor that keep it from block and silt. Nevertheless, we cannot praise enough the creative work of the people at the times without precise equipments and mechanics. There is nothing we can say but that it is among the miracles in the history of the building industry.

60. The Former Imperial Palace without Chimney or Toilet

When admiring the ancient magnificent complex of the former Imperial Palace, one might be wonder why there were no chimneys or toilets in such a large area. They must like to know how the heating system was set in the palaces. As we understand, the buildings in the Forbidden City are basically in wood-and-brick structure, so it can easily cause a fire. Just for that reason, the emperors of successive dynasties paid much attention to the use of fire in the Palace.

The careful visitors may find a wooden cover in one meter square on the floor in each of the corridors of the palaces. These

were just the mouths of the flues constructed below the corridors, which lead directly to that beneath the floor paved with the high quality gold-like bricks of the halls and palaces. In every year, around the days of Hoarfrost Descends (the 18th of the 24 solar terms), large stoves were lit in the fire ducts by the eunuchs in charge of such things, so even heating air baked the floor of the palaces constantly. This elaborate heating system is similar to the *Kang* (the hollow brick bed warmed by a fire lit below) of the countryside in north area of China.

Aside from the fire duct beneath the floor, fire pans, or braziers could also provide heating in winter. These exquisite braziers were usually covered with a metal mesh for preventing sparks flying out. Some of them are gilt bronze and some are cloisonné enamel. The larger ones weigh 500 kg or more, and the smaller ones are easily portable. At present, these kinds of refined braziers are still preserved in the three great halls and three rear palaces as well as in the Hall of Mental Cultivation and six western palaces. In addition, the braziers were also designed as hand or foot warmers specifically used by the emperor and his empress and concubines. Owing to the elaborate heating facilities, even in the coldest days of the strong north wind whistling in winter, it was still as warm as in the spring day when staying in the warmed-palaces.

During the Ming and Qing period, charcoal was the ideal fuel to be used in cooking or heating by reason that it did not produce peculiar smell or strong smoke-rising when burring. In other words, it didn't cause air pollution, so the Forbidden City was not in need of the chimney.

In former imperial palace, another strange thing is that there was no toilet in the old days. From the emperor, empress and concubines to court ladies and eunuchs, all the people who lived in the palace used chamber-pots instead of using toilets. Excreted faeces and urine were cleaned with charcoal ash and transported outside of the Forbidden City by eunuchs who were responsible for sanitation works in the palace. The charcoal ash used as the cleaning material not only eliminated the bad smell, but also absorbed the moisture. It's indeed a wonderful thing, making use of waste material.

61. Glass Windows in the Imperial Palace

Plate glass used for doors or windows began to be produced in China in the late Qing Dynasty, but according to the record of the history documents, the windowpanes had appeared in the palace long before that period. In that case, when were the windows of the palaces fixed with glass? And where did the glass come from? In some ancient records, we learned that windowpanes were fixed in the first year of the Emperor Yongzheng's reign (1723), from which we can infer that windowpanes that appeared in the palace couldn't be later than the period of Yongzheng, and it's much possible in the more earlier period of Kangxi's reign.

All the plate glass used at that time came from Europe, such as France, Holland, Italy, etc. In the early days of Yongzheng— Qianlong period, the windowpanes used in the palace were quite small in size, because they were a considerable expense and large pans of glass were also quite a rare thing; thus, only smaller panes could be fixed in the central window lattice and the other lattices were still pasted with paper. This method was vividly called "to set up the glass-eye of window".

With the daily increase of imported glass, more buildings in the palace could use it instead of the paper. From the middle or late of Qianlong's reign, the using of windowpanes appeared in a whole window, not in one or two lattices in the center of it as before, but the lack of the large plate glass during that time, some windowpanes were joined with several smaller pieces. When there was large enough glass to set up in the whole window, the window lattices were naturally cut off.

The plate glass imported at that time was extremely expensive. One square meter glass was equal to more than 15 taels of fine silver, that is enough grain to be eaten in one year by seven people. According to the price of a house at that time, the price of two windowpanes was equivalent to that of one room. So, as we know, when the plate glass was introduced into China, except the imperial palaces, gardens, and a few of mansions of princes, no common people, even the general officials could afford it.

62. Fire Prevention in Yesterday's Palace

Traditional Chinese buildings are mainly timber structures. Fire threat is the greatest of all. In the history of the Forbidden City, more than 10 big fires were recorded, each time brought serious damages to the palace. For the emperors who had lived in the city, the more threat was facing, the more attention had been paid to cope with it.

God was a certain resort at that time. Inside the imperial garden, a building located in the middle enclosure walls is the temple of Daoism. The God of water had been enshrined inside for a long time. The location of the temple itself reflects the importance of the building and of the god. Besides, decorative tile components on the building roof, such as main ridge end decors of dragon motif, small decorative figures in row on flying hip ridges are all used to frighten away the evil of fire. *Wenyuange* (Pavilion of Source of literature) is another example that adopts colors of water according to traditional beliefs to overwhelm fires.

Daily care is the most import of all, especially in the years when flames were burning in the lamp to give light at night. Just as emperor Kangxi ordered his servants, "Light is the key problem. Every place of light must be guarded. No absence is forgivable. Chiefs have the duty of frequent inspection." Every day when dusk was coming, eunuchs voices could be heard now and then, "Down load door bolt, lock, and take care of lights."

In case of fires that took place, there were also devices to extinguish them. 300 giant vats placed inside the Forbidden City were not only for decorative purposes, but also for storing water to put off fires. During winter time, eunuchs from the Imperial Household Department were responsible for coating the vats with cotton covers, capping them, and making the fire at the bottom to prevent freezing. Thick incrustations can still be seen in some vats.

A fire brigade was organized during emperor Kangxi's reign for better fireproof. The members were all eunuchs who went their rounds for looking after the candles and lamps and were equipped with an old fire extinguisher, *Jitong*. *Jitong* is a kind of water thrower, maybe made after a western device. Historic archives show that all the guards from Eight Banners had their fire brigades who were on duty to protect the Forbidden City, and were trained at ordinary times. It was recorded too that each sub-brigade from one of the Eight Banner guards was responsible for the safety of an assigned area of the imperial palace. When a place outside the Forbidden City but inside the Imperial City was on fire, sub-brigades were to be sent from every banner to work together. As reformation took place in the 31st year of emperor Guangxu's reign, an imperial edict was issued, ordering to establish a Police Ministry and a Police Center in Beijing. The fire department was under the control of the Police Center. From then on, the department was responsible for the fires in the outskirts of the Forbidden City, and a fire brigade of around 100 people remained to guard the imperial palaces. By the time when the last emperor Puyi abdicated, the troop had yet 50 men or so.

63. The Guard of the Forbidden City

Emperors of all dynasties regarded their living palace as forbidden areas and they were guarded strictly. Walls of 10 meters in height were built around the Forbidden City and there was a city moat of 50 meters in width around the walls. Between the inside ban of city moat and the wall a tight guarding system was set up. In Ming dynasty 40 *Hong Pu* (Red *Pu*, a duty station of three rooms) had been built. Ten soldiers and officer stationed at each *Hong Pu* were on duty 24 hours round. From dusk till dawn, bells started to ring at the first *Hong Pu* at *Queyou* Gate, and then transferred to the next *Hong Pu* around the forbidden wall one by one. 20 generals were in their night shift every 2 hours around the forbidden wall. 8 patrol officers toured along east and west direction separately. The patrol officers inspected their tally mutually while they met, and then the patrol routine would be continued. In the Qing dynasty, unlike the former rule, the periphery of the Forbidden City was guarded by the lower five banner troops of Eight Banner Army. The way of ringing the bell was changed into to passing wooden cudgel. Every night started from the counting of the night clappers, a piece of wooden cudgel, one feet in length was delivered from the start point of *Quezuo* Gate through one *Hong Pu* to another, and to be transmitted back and forth till dawn of the next morning. The patrol and stationed guards were not only along the periphery of the Forbidden City, but also executed within the palace. In the Forbidden City, the guarding duty was divided into several districts, the patrol guarding troops rang the bell or transmitted wooden cudgel during their duty time. Until the middle age of Qing dynasty, in order to further strengthen the guarding system, 736 rooms were built along the city moat inner bank and surrounding city wall to allow the Forbidden City to be more tightly guarded.

Four gates of the Forbidden City were heavily guarded too. In Qing dynasty, two red canes were set at each gate wielded by two palace guards. Anyone who entered the gate without authorization and if their name had not been reported should be beaten by the red cane. Outside of each gate of the Forbidden City, there were steles with the characters "Dismount the horse" scripted at both left and right side. Except those who had the emperor's special permission, anyone came to the stele, the civil officers had to get out from their sedan and the military officers had to get down from horse to enter the palace on foot.

The Forbidden City was so heavily guarded that in the feudal time civilians were unable to go near to the imperial palace at all. Even the high-ranking ministers could not enter the Forbidden City without authorization. Personnel of imperial court who were to come in and get out the Forbidden City was required to have special credentials. There were two kinds of such credentials. One was called *Hefu* and the other was *Yaopai*.

Hefu was a special pass. It was used for the ones who needed it for emergencies to pass through the forbidden gates. *Hefu* was made from bronze in two opposing pieces. Two pieces formed a set, there were two words, *Shengzhi* (imperial edict) cast on both piece in convex and concave shape separately. The piece of concave shape casting words was administered by the officer who guarded the gate. The other piece in convex casting words was held within the palace. If there was some one under the decree in the night or there was some emergency military affairs needed to pass the palace gate, one had to hold the *Hefu* in convex casting words to the gate. The guard of the gate took out the other piece of *Hefu* with concave casting words that he administered, combined with that one came from the inner palace. If two pieces match well, then the holder of the *Hefu* could pass, and be registered and reported to the emperor the day after. If the two pieces did not match each other, through would not be permitted.

Yao pai was a temporary pass issued to the palace corvee by the Minister of Internal Affairs. This kind of pass was hung up on the waist so it was called *Yaopai*, literally waist tally. The palace usually hired different kinds of corvee, such as cooking corvee, craftsman corvee and sundry corvee. The minister of internal affairs ascertained the life experience and background of each corvee, and each had to have their own guarantor. The name, age, birthplace, facial features and job were all listed in detail before a *Yaopai* was issued. Such a detailed list was copied and one was collected in the minister of internal affairs, and the other one was delivered to *Donghuamen*, *Xihuamen*, *Longzongmen*, and *Jingyunmen* duty offices for inspection when a corvee went through the gates. Imperial court stipulated that all the *Yaopai* be used by the corvee exclusively, lending it out to others would result in a serious punishment.

There were troops in all their force guarding around the Forbidden City. Any person would be interrogated and questioned by guarding troops while passing through the palace gates. Such was the Forbidden City strongly fortified, but accidents also happened when someone passed through under false pretences. In the 8th year of the Jiaqing period, Chen De, a common person who hid a knife and snuck into *Donghuamen*, and reached the place between *Shenwumen* and *Shunzhenmen*. When emperor Jiaqing was passing through *Shunzhenmen*, Chen De appeared and assassinated the emperor by the knife, but he was hopelessly outnumbered and arrested. Chen De was put to death by the sternest punishment of body dismembering. From then on, the forbidden gates were more tightly guarded.

64. The Displays of Original Conditions

The Former Imperial Palace was the residence of the 24 emperors of both Ming and Qing Dynasties, known as the Forbidden City. Visitors can review the scenes of the luxurious and extravagant life of the imperial family and understand the related political customs of the past years. The Palace Museum opened some halls and palaces under their original conditions, such as the three front halls, the three rear palaces, and a part of the west palaces as well.

Raised on a three-layered terrace of white marble, the three front halls was the center of the outer court: *Taihedian* (Hall of Great Harmony), *Zhonghedian* (Hall of Middle Harmony) and

Baohedian (Hall of Preserving Harmony), among which, *Taihedian*, also called *"Jinluandian"* (Hall of Imperial Throne), with a double-eaved roof, is the highest-ranking and the largest one in the extant ancient Chinese architecture. Covering 2,377 square meters and paved with gold-like-bricks, *Taihedian* is 35 meters high and has 72 columns. A caisson with coiled dragon relief converged in the center of the ceiling. The imperial throne is set on a platform of the golden lacquer, surrounded with a same lacquered screen carved with dragon design, on both side of which stand six gilt pillars entwined with coiling dragons. The grand ceremonies were held in the hall on special occasions, like the lunar New Year, Winter solstice, the emperor's birthday, ascending the throne, conferring the empress title, the grand court audiences, etc.

Zhonghedian (Hall of Middle Harmony) has a pointed roof. Before going to *Taihedian* to attend the ceremony, the emperor

first came here for a rest and received the obeisances from the officials in charge of the ceremony. In addition, when the time of the emperor wanted to do worships to the Temple of Heaven, Temple of Earth, or the Temple of Imperial Ancestors, the emperor would come here to read the worship articles.

Baohedian (Hall of Preserving Harmony), with a double-eaved roof in the hip and gables type, was the place where Qing emperors held banquets in honor of princes and dukes of Mongolia and ministers. It was also the site of the "Palace Examination" (the highest one in the feudal imperial examination) of the Qing Dynasty, which was held once every three years. The emperor himself set the exam paper for the examinees and he himself even marked for the first ten participants. The top three ones in such examination were respectively called Zhuangyuan (No. 1 scholar), Bangyan (No. 2 scholar) and Tanhua (No. 3 scholar).

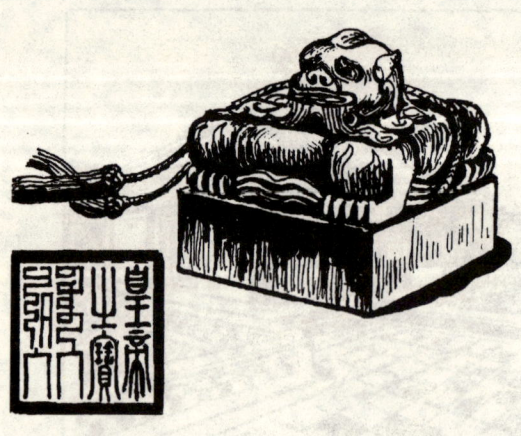

Over the Hall of Preserving Harmony and through *Qianqingmen* (Gate of Heavenly Purity), is *Qianqinggong* (Palace of Heavenly Purity), in which 14 Ming and the early Qing emperor Shunzhi and Kangxi lived. The emperors also dealt with routine affairs at this palace. Right above the throne, behind the horizontal tablet with four characters, *Zheng Da Guang Ming* (means upright and aboveboard), a small case kept the secret testament (decree) on succession to the Qing throne. After the emperor passed away, the case would be opened by the pointed minister, and according to the decree in the case, the one who had been selected by the pre-emperor would be the successor to the throne.

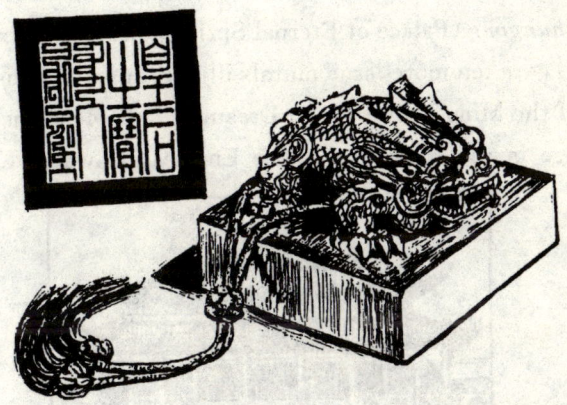

Immediately behind *Qianqinggong* (Hall of Heavenly Purity) is *Jiaotaidian* (Hall of Union), where 25 imperial seals are kept. There is also a clepsydra (an ancient water clock) and a mechanical clock on display.

Kunninggong (Palace of Earthly Tranquility) was the

normal bedchamber of the empress in the Ming Dynasty, and later, it was made into a place for worshipping the Gods according to the customs of the Manchu, only leaving the east side room as the emperor's nuptial chamber. Now, the furnishings in the room remain to be exactly the same as those of the Emperor Guangxu's wedding ceremony.

The six western palaces were the living quarters of the concubines. *Chuxiugong*, among of which (Palace of Gathering Excellence) was where the Empress Dowager Cixi once lived and gave the birth in the rear hall to her son, named Zaichun, who became the later Emperor Tongzhi. At present, the interior of the palace reflects its original conditions of Empress Dowager Cixi's 50th birthday celebrations. On the walls of the corridors of *Changchungong* (Palace of Eternal Spring, one of the six western palaces), are ten more large murals illustrating a famous Chinese novel of the Ming Dynasty, "A Dream of Red Mansions". There is a stage in the courtyard. The Empress Dowager Cixi often

enjoyed operas when she lived here.

To the south of the six western palaces is *Yangxindian* (Hall of Mental Cultivation). From the Emperor Yongzheng, a total of eight Qing emperors once lived here. The side room was also where the Empress Dowager took charge of the state affairs behind a curtain. Two thrones for emperor and empress dowager were separated by a yellow curtain. The east side room was a place for emperor to handle state affairs and made audiences to his grand councilors of the state. At the end of the suite of the west room is a small study room named *Sanxitang* (Room of Three Rarities), because the Emperor Qianlong once collected here his three very famous calligraphy of Jin Dynasty—*Kuai Xue Shi Qing Tie* (Clear Sky after Pleasant Snow) of Wang Xizhi, *Zhong Qiu Tie* (Mid-Autumn) of Wang Xianzhi, and *Bo Yuan Tie* of Wang Xun.

On December 12, 1912, the Empress Dowager Longyu, in the Hall of Mental Cultivation, issued the imperial edict of abdication, closing the reign of the Qing Dynasty.

65. The Special Exhibition Halls

As the largest Museum in the whole country, The Palace Museum houses nearly one million pieces of precious historical cultural relics.

In order that the broad masses of visitors may see the treasures of ancient arts with their own eyes and learn the history and culture of a long standing Chinese nation, the Palace Museum has opened some special exhibition halls, which are respectively introduced as follows:

Zhenbao Guan (Hall of Jewelry)

The Hall of Jewelry is housed in *Hangjidian* (Hall of Imperial Supremacy) and *Ningshougong* (Palace of Tranquility and Longevity). On display here are mainly the Qing court collections: gold and silver wares, jewelry, precious articles of daily use, luxurious adornments, and exquisite artworks used by imperial family members or set out in their living palaces, which include imperial gold seal, gold title-scroll, Ruyi-scepters of different materials, gold pagoda made of 3,000-odd tales of gold for preserving hairs of Emperor Qianlong's mother, Empress Dowager Chongqing; and furthermore, the well-made emperor's armor linked up with more than 600 thousands small steel sheets, the summer sleeping mat woven with ivory strips, and the Jade-hill with the weight of 5,350 kilograms carved with a scene of Da Yu (the reputed founder of the Xia Dynasty c. 21st-16th century BC) Controlling Flood.

Zhongbiao Guan (Hall of Clocks and Watches)

The Hall of Clocks and Watches is housed in *Fengxiandian* (Hall of Worshipping Ancestors). A variety of clocks and watches once collected in the Qing court are on display here. Except for some pieces that were made in Guangzhou and the Clock-making workshop of the Qing court, a lot of them came from England, France, and Switzerland. These timepieces not only vary in shape, but in methods of giving the correct time. All the gorgeous decorations on the clocks and watches, such as blooming flowers, dancing butterflies, walking figures, flowing water, the melodious music, and sweet birds singing, will fire any visitors fantastic imagination.

Qingtongqi Guan （The Hall of Bronzes）

The east gallery of Qianqinggong (Palace of Heavenly Purity) now is the Hall of Bronzes. More than 500 bronzes ranging from the Shang Dynasty (16th – 11th century BC) to the Warring States period (475 – 221 BC) are exhibited here. From these magnificent and exquisite bronzes, visitors can find the food containers, wine vessels, ritual wares, weapons, and ornaments of chariot and harness. The splendid bronze-culture created by ancient Chinese people is highly rated by domestic and foreign scholars and visitors.

Taoci Guan （The Hall of Ceramics）

The Hall of Ceramics is housed in the west gallery of Qianqinggong. As the homeland of the ceramics, painted pottery articles appeared as early as 6,000 years ago in China. Primitive porcelain and celadon wares were successively matured in the Shang Dynasty (c. 16th – 11th century BC) and East Han Dynasty

(25 - 220 AD). From then on, pottery and porcelain of our country have more and more improvements with the lapse of time. Here you can see the painted pottery articles of Yangshao culture, black pottery of Longshan culture, the primitive porcelain of Shang and Zhou Dynasties, Bluish white porcelain of the Wei (226 - 265 AD) and Jin (265 - 420 AD) Dynasties, the famous tri-colored glazed pottery of the Tang Dynasty (618 - 907 AD); the *Ru*, *Ge*, *Guan*, *Ding* and *Jun* wares of the Song Dynasty (960 - 1279 AD), and other exquisite wares made in Jingdezhen during the period of Yuan (1279 - 1368), Ming (1368 - 1644) and Qing (1644 - 1911) Dynasties.

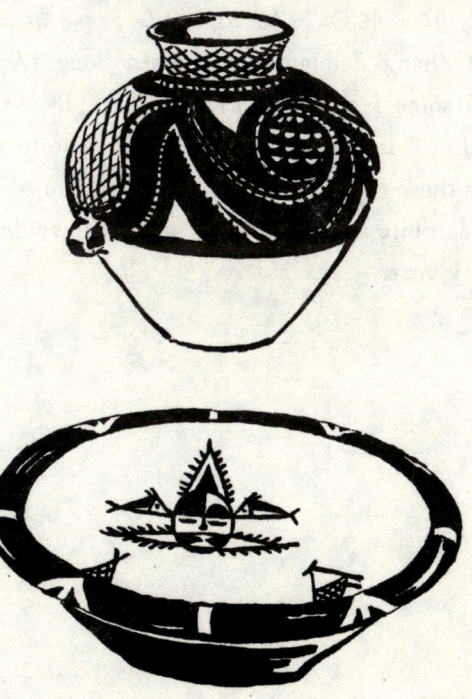

Huihua Guan （Hall of Paintings）

The Hall of Paintings is housed in the west gallery of *Baohedian* （Hall of Preserving Harmony）. More than 100 thousand paintings and calligraphy ranging from Jin （265 – 420 AD) to Qing （1644 – 1911) Dynasties are collected in the Palace Museum. In October, the finest season of Beijing, the master pieces would be selected for display here in turn, such as *Traveling in Spring* by Zhan Ziqian of Sui Dynasty （581 – 618), *Emperor Taizong in a Sedan Chair Greeting An Envoy from Tibet* by Yan Liben and *Five Oxen* by Han Huang of Tang Dynasty （618 – 907), *Han Xizai's Night Revels* by Gu Hongzhong of Five Dynasties （907 – 960), *The Riverside Scene at the Qingming Festival* by Zhang Zeduan of Northern Song Dynasty （960 – 1127), and some famous works of calligraphy written by Yan Zhenqing, Liu Gongquan, Ouyang Xun and so forth.

Besides these exhibition halls above mentioned, some special temporary exhibitions on different subjects would be held for visitors every year.

66. The Unopened Areas of the Imperial Palace

Since the Palace Museum was set up on the 10th of October in 1925, the world-renowned ancient architecture complex and its cultural relics have been well preserved and utilized. Up to now, most areas of the Imperial Palace have been opened to the public, such as the three front halls, the three rear palaces, the inner eastern section, the inner western section, and the outer eastern section, as well as 10-odd special exhibition halls have also opened one after another. There are still some places in the Forbidden City that remain unopened. They are as follows:

Wenhuadian (Hall of Literary Glory)

Wenhuadian, originally built in the Ming Dynasty, stands in the east part of outer court. At first, it was only an ordinary place where the emperor often came, but later, it turned into a site specially used for listening to lectures and holding banquets. During the Emperor Guangxu's reign, it was once a spot to receive the foreign envoys. Behind *Wenhuadian* is the *Wenyuange* (Pavilion of Source of Literature) in which the S*i Ku Quan Shu* (Complete Library in Four Division) was stored.

Wuyingdian 〔Hall of Military Eminences〕

Standing symmetrically to the *Wenhua Dian*, inside the *Xihuamen* (West Glory Gate) is *Wuyingdian*, where the emperor once lived and summoned officials in the early Ming Dynasty. In addition, Li Zicheng, the leader of the peasant uprising army of the late Ming period, also dealt with the state affairs here after he occupied the Forbidden City. During and after the period of the Qing Emperor Qianlong, it became a place for printing books. All the books compiled and printed here were called the imperial-edition book.

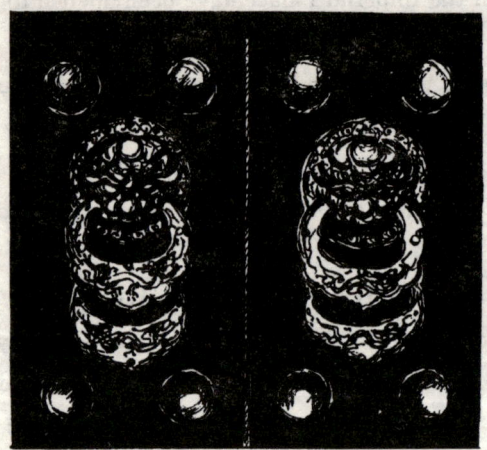

Outer west section

The outer west section was the place where the widows of the late emperor lived and worshiped Buddha. This section includes *Ci'ninggong* (Palace of Compassion and Tranquility), *Ci'ninggong* Garden, *Shoukanggong* (Palace of Longevity and

Well-Being), *Shouan'gong* (Palace of Tranquil and Tranquility) and *Yinghuadian* (Hall of Exuberance), etc. Among them the *Ci'ninggong* Garden has the unique style comparing with other gardens in the Forbidden City.

Yuhuage (Yu Hua Pavilion)

On the southwest of the Forbidden City stands the Rain Flower Pavilion, a three-storied building. Gilt-bronze tiles on the roof and huge flying dragons separately crouching along the four ridges look more magnificent and vivid. Here was once the place for worshipping the Gods of Tibetan Lamaism. On the days of the 8th in the 2nd, 3rd and 4th lunar months every year, Lamas would be asked to chant sutras in each story of the building.

Yuqinggong (Palace of Crowned Prince)

Outside the *Jingyunmen* (Gate of Great Fortune), and inside the *Qianxing* Gate, is *Yuqinggong*, in which the crown princes of the Qing Dynasty once lived and studied. The structure of the room-partitions in this palace was very complicated and changeable. So it is also called "labyrinthine palace". Anyone who enters the palace would easily lose his way.

Yanxigong (Palace of Prolonged Happiness)

The palace of Prolonged Happiness is one of the six eastern palaces. In its courtyard, there is a special building commonly known as the "Crystal Palace". It got its name because it was constructed with steel and copper beams and columns, covered with glasses and surrounded with clear water.

Nansansuo (Three South Residences)

Three south residences, with the *Xiefangdian* (Hall of Gathering Fragrance) as the center, covered with green glazed tiles on the roofs, were the living quarter for the Qing princes before they were apointed the crown prince. The buildings including Taiyiyuan (Imperial Hospital), Yuyaoku (Imperial Drug Store) and Huidian'guan (Hall for Collection of the Records of Laws and Systems) also belong to the Three south residences.

Beiwusuo (Five North Residences)

The Five north residences, lying to the east of *Qianqinggong*, were mainly composed of Jingshifang (Eunuch Office), Sizhiku, Gudongfang (Antiquities Store), Shouyaofang (Storehouse of Medicines for Prolonging Life), and *Ruyi* Hall. At first, the complex was also the living quarter of the Qing princes.

Jianfugong (Palace of Establishing Happiness) Garden

In the southwest area of the Forbidden City was originally the *Jianfugong* Garden, where elegant winding corridors crossing the broad yard and splendid towers alternating with noble pavilions presented an extremely peaceful and quiet scenery. Unfortunately, the beautiful garden was destroyed by a disastrous fire at night on June 26, 1923. There only remains a scene of ruins and rubbles.

The Rear Part of Qianlong Garden

Qianlong Garden contains four sections. At present, only the front part including *Guhuaxuan* (Pavilion of Ancient Glory), and *Suichutang* (Hall of Fulfilling Original Wishes) is open to the public. The other two scenic spots are still in close, mainly including the *Cuishanglou* (Tower for Viewing Beautiful Scenery), *Juanqinzhai* (Lodge for Retired Life), *Biluoting* (Pavilion of Jade-Green Couch Shell), *Fuwangge* (Pavilion of the Anticipation of Good Fortune), and so forth.

In order that the splendid palatial complex can be opened to public as early as possible, the preparations for the restoration are well underway.

67. Preservation and Utilization of the Imperial Palace

It can't be but considered really a miracle that the Forbidden City, a residence of 24 emperors of Ming and Qing Dynasties, could be preserved completely after dozens of warring years. This miracle is created by those who devoted their endeavors even their lives to the preservation of the great cultural heritage.

In 1911, the Xinhai Revolution smashed the rule of the Qing Dynasty, but the Qing imperial family members still lived in the rear part of the Forbidden City according to the terms of preferential treatment, while the outer court belonged to the new government. In 1914, the Antiquity Museum was founded. Some culture relics from the imperial palace in Shenyang and the summer residence in Chengde were on displays in three great halls, the *Wuyingdian* (Hall of Military Eminences) and

Wenhuadian (Hall of Literary Glory). In 1924, the abdicated emperor Puyi was driven out from the Forbidden City. In the same year, *Shanweihui*, the Committee of Dealing with the Affairs Left Over by The Qing Court was established. It was mainly responsible for checking up the property of the Qing court. At its first meeting, the Committee made the decision to set up the Palace Museum in the following year. In the course of the checking-work, the Committee stood up against the disturbances and pressure from the warlords, the turbulence government, and the old fogies of the abdication Qing Dynasty. In October 10,1925, the Palace Museum was established. It first opened the rear middle section and the west section of the Imperial Palace to the public, such as the three rear palaces, Imperial Garden and six western palaces, as well as *Yangxindian* (Hall of Mental Cultivation), *Shou'an'gong* (Palace of Longevity and Tranquility), *Wenyuan'ge* (Pavilion of Literary Source) and *Leshoutang* (Hall of Pleasure and Longevity). From then on, the leaders of the Palace Museum Li Yuying and Yi Peiji, and other celebrities including well-known figures of various circles all did their utmost for the safety and preservation of the Imperial Palace. Until 1947, the turmoil situation of the Palace Museum was stable. It took over the Antiquity Museum and opened the whole Imperial Palace.

On the eve of the War of Resistance Against Japan, for protection the cultural heritage of the Qing court from being destroyed by the war, a great deal of cultural relics and archives turned over to Shanghai and Nanjing, then to Sichuan and Guizhou. After the victory of the War of Resistance Against

Japan, a part of cultural relics was sent back to Beijing, and the rest was transported to Taiwan.

When the abdication emperor Puyi left the Imperial Palace, except *Yangxindian* (Hall of Mental Cultivation), *Chuxiugong* (Palace of Gathering Excellence), *Changchungong* (Palace of Eternal Spring), *Zhongcuigong* (Palace of Gathering Essence) and *Yonghegong* (Palace of Eternal Harmony), other palaces and halls were rather old and shabby. Although having several renovations with donations after the Palace Museum was set up in 1925, the once magnificent and brilliant Imperial Palace still presented a scene of decay and desolations when it was reopened to the public in 1947.

Up to the liberation of Beijing, the Imperial Palace was really given a new life. The government has attached importance to the preservation and renovation of the Imperial Palace. Actually, since 1958, the Palace Museum has never ceased the project of renovation. Furthermore, some new installations have also been added, such as power-supply system, heating facilities, cesspipe, drainage ditch and etc, thus giving a new look to the 570 year-old palaces. During the period of the Culture Revolution, the Palace Museum was once closed for the sake of safety. In addition, the Palace Museum has spared no efforts or cost on purchasing scattered relics at home and abroad. More than one million pieces of cultural relics now have been collected in the Museum.

Today, as an institution for academic research, the Palace Museum has played an important role both in the study of Chinese history and the ancient artistic fields.

68. How to Visit the Palace Museum?

Covering 720,000 square meters with almost 9,000 rooms, the Forbidden City is a huge place. Aside from the splendid ancient architectures, the Palace Museum has sponsored more than ten special exhibitions and temporary shows for the viewers. With so many scenic spots and interesting displays, how can you appreciate all the treasures?

Now, here are some suggestions for your reference only.

If you are a person with wide-interest or if you have a plenty of time, we hope that you can visit as many spots as possible with a close look at every individual object, building and its history. First, you

can read the plan and introduction to the Imperial Palace at both the south and north gates, then, according to the location of the palaces and halls decide your visit route. Moreover, a lot of signposts and a variety of plans installed at the major road, crossings and squares can help you find your way around easily.

If you are interested in the displays under the original palace conditions, but don't have enough time for all the complex, you may completely leave out the special exhibitions and just visit the three front halls, three rear palaces and the six western palaces. If possible, you can also come to the Hall of Jewelry for the jewelries on display are closely related to the imperial family's life.

If you are just a lover of the ancient arts, you could spend more time appreciating the special exhibitions of ancient paintings, bronzes, ceramics, jade wares and so on. The tremendous amount of gems of ancient Chinese art will be most fascinating.

You can also visit the imperial palace with all the convenient services. The Palace Museum has supplied a series of services for you. At the ticket office, you can buy a small guidebook that will guide you to the sights of the palaces. Meanwhile, there are also some introduction boards at the halls and the palaces that can give you the details you want. The wired broadcast station of the Palace Museum gives you a special program, "Introduction to the Palace Museum" regularly. The tape-recorded guide is also available to you in more than ten languages, such as *Putonghua* (the standard Chinese pronunciation), Guangdong dialect, Chaozhou dialect, as well as English, French, German, Japanese, etc. This can be rented at the south gate and returned at the north gate. Furthermore, in the opened areas of the Forbidden City, several hundreds of our staff members are ready to answer your questions and help you in every way.

Appendix

Names of Main Halls and Palaces in the Forbidden City

1. 午 门   *Wumen*   Meridian Gate
2. 内金水桥   *Neijinshuiqiao*   The lnner Golden River Bridges
3. 熙和门   *Xihemen*   Gate of Glorious Harmony
4. 协和门   *Xiehemen*   Gate of Unified Harmony
5. 太和门   *Taihemen*   Gate of Great Harmony
6. 文华殿   *Wenhuadian*   Hall of Literary Glory
7. 文渊阁   *Wenyuan'ge*   Pavilion of Source of Literature
8. 武英殿   *Wuyingdian*   Hall of Military Eminences
9. 东华门   *Donghuamen*   East Glorious Gate
10. 西华门   *Xihuamen*   Vest Glorious Gate
11. 弘义阁   *Hongyige*   Pavilion of Glorying Righteousness
12. 体仁阁   *Tiren'ge*   Pavilion of State Benevolence
13. 太和殿   *Taihedian*   Hall of Great Harmony
14. 中和殿   *Zhonghedian*   Hall of Middle Harmony

15.	保和殿	*Baohedian*	Hall of Preserving Harmony
16.	箭 亭	*Jianting*	Arrow Pavilion
17.	御膳房	*Yushanfang*	The Imperial Kitchen
18.	南三所	*Nansansuo*	Three South Residences
19.	乾清门	*Qianqingmen*	Gate of Heavenly Purity
20.	隆宗门	*Longzongmen*	Gate of Great Ancestors
21.	景运门	*Jingyunmen*	Gate of Great Fortune
22.	乾清宫	*Qianqinggong*	Palace of Heavenly Purity
23.	交泰殿	*Jiaotaidian*	Hall of Union
24.	坤宁宫	*Kunninggong*	Hall of Earthly Tranquility
25.	坤宁门	*Kunningmen*	Gate of Earthly Tranquility
26.	御花园	*Yuhuayuan*	Imperial Garden
27.	钦安殿	*Qin'andian*	Hall of Imperial Peace
28.	绛雪轩	*Jiangxuexuan*	Pavillion of Crimson Snow
29.	养性斋	*Yangxingzhai*	Studio of Character Cultivation
30.	钟粹宫	*Zhongcuigong*	Palace of Gathering Essence
31.	景阳宫	*Jingyanggong*	Hall of Great *Yang*
32.	承乾宫	*Chengqian'gong*	Palace of Inheriting Heaven
33.	永和宫	*Yonghegong*	Palace of Eternal Harmony
34.	景仁宫	*Jingren'gong*	Palace of Great Benevolence
35.	延禧宫	*Yanxigong*	Palace of Prolonged Happiness
36.	诚肃殿	*Chengsudian*	Sincere and Respectful Hall
37.	斋 宫	*Zhaigong*	Palace of Abstinence
38.	奉先殿	*Fengxiandian*	Hall of Worshipping Ancestors
39.	锡庆门	*Xiqingmen*	Gate of Bestowing

			Happiness
40.	九龙壁	*Jiulongbi*	Nine-Dragon Screen
41.	皇极门	*Huangjimen*	Gate of lmperial Supremacy
42.	宁寿门	*Ningshoumen*	Gate of Tranquility and Longevity
43.	皇极殿	*Huangjidian*	Hall of lmperial Supremacy
44.	宁寿宫	*Ningshougong*	Palace of Tranquility and Longevity
45.	畅音阁	*Changyin'ge*	Pavilion of Pleasant Sounds
46.	养性殿	*Yangxingdian*	Hall of Cultivating Nature
47.	乐寿堂	*Leshoutang*	Hall of Pleasure and Longevity
48.	颐和轩	*Yihexuan*	Pavilion of Well-nourished Harmony
49.	珍妃井	*Zhenfeijing*	Concubine Zhen Well
50.	宁寿宫花园	*Ningshougong Huayuan*	Ning Shou Gong Garden (or Qianlong Garden)
51.	贞顺门	*Zhenshunmen*	Gate of Truth and Compliance
52.	咸福宫	*Xianfugong*	Palace of Complete Happiness
53.	储秀宫	*Chuxiugong*	Palace of Gathering Excellence
54.	长春宫	*Changchungong*	Palace of Eternal Spring
55.	体和殿	*Tihedian*	Hall of State Harmony
56.	翊坤宫	*Yikungong*	Palace of Blessings to Mother Earth
57.	体元殿	*Tiyuandian*	Hall of State Unity

58.	太极殿	*Taijidian*	Hall of Great Supremacy
59.	永寿宫	*Yongshougong*	Palace of Eternal Longevity
60.	养心殿	*Yangxindian*	Hall of Mental Cultivation
61.	军机处	*Junjichu*	The Grand Council of State
62.	雨华阁	*Yuhuage*	Yu Hua Pavilion
63.	英华殿	*Yinghuadian*	Hall of Exuberance
64.	寿安宫	*Shou'an'gong*	Palace of Longevity and Tranquility
65.	寿康宫	*Shoukanggong*	Palace of Longevity and Well-Being
66.	慈宁宫	*Ci'ninggong*	Palace of Compassion and Tranquility
67.	慈宁宫花园	*Ci'ninggong huayuan*	Ci Ning Gong Garden
68.	角　楼	*Jiaolou*	Corner Tower
	角　楼	*Jiaolou*	Corner Tower
	角　楼	*Jiaolou*	Corner Tower
	角　楼	*Jiaolou*	Corner Tower
69.	顺贞门	*Shunzhenmen*	Gate of Pursuit and Truth
70.	神武门	*Shenwumen*	Gate of Martial Spirit